A CHEETAH'S
TALE

A CHEETAH'S TALE

HER ROYAL HIGHNESS
PRINCESS MICHAEL OF KENT

BRADT

First published in the UK in September 2017
by Bradt Travel Guides Ltd
IDC House, The Vale, Chalfont St Peter, Bucks SL9 9RZ, England
www.bradtguides.com
Reprinted January 2018

Text copyright © 2017 HRH Princess Michael of Kent
Photographs copyright © 2017 Individual photographers *see page 207*
Edited by Caroline Taggart
Proofread by Janet Mears
Designed & typeset from the author's files by Ian Spick, Bradt & Dataworks
Cover design by Pepi Bluck
Cover photograph: HRH Princess Michael of Kent with cheetah cub © John Swannell
Reproduction & colour work: Fiona Cox at Creative Design & Print (Stamford) Ltd
Production managed by Sue Cooper, Bradt & Jellyfish Print Solutions

ISBN: 978 1 78477 069 3 (print)
e-ISBN: 978 1 78477 515 5 (e-pub)
e-ISBN: 978 1 78477 416 5 (mobi)

British Library Cataloguing in Publication Data
A catalogue record for this book is available from the British Library

Printed in the UK
Digital conversion by www.dataworks.co.in

CONTENTS

To Lente Roode and Laurie Marker
My Cheetah Muses and my constant inspiration

FOREWORD

BY JONATHAN AND ANGELA SCOTT

Watching a cheetah sprinting across the savannah speaks of a perfectly evolved predator operating at the height of its powers, a thing of exquisite beauty and grace, testimony to the ingenuity of nature. However, this fastest of land mammals is running into trouble. Why?

Studies in the 1980s highlighted how vulnerable cheetah cubs are to predation from lions and hyenas, which sometimes kill whole litters. Mother cheetahs den among long grass, dense reedbeds or impenetrable thickets. So whenever cover is in short supply, as it is on the Serengeti Plains, cub mortality can be as high as 95 per cent. Contrast this with the situation on game and cattle ranches in Namibia, where the vast majority of the country's estimated 1,500 cheetahs are found. Over time farmers and ranchers have systematically eradicated lions, hyenas and leopards with guns, traps and poison, inadvertently enabling cheetah populations to increase in the absence of their more numerous and aggressive competitors, with litters of three or more cubs not uncommonly raised to independence. This illustrates that, despite concerns raised by scientists in the 1980s about low levels of genetic variability, cheetahs have no inherent problem breeding. Difficulties experienced in captive facilities are likely to be a reflection of the fact that males and females meet infrequently in the wild and more than one male may father cubs in a single litter, conditions not easily replicated in captivity.

Thanks to the long-term studies of the Serengeti Cheetah Project in Tanzania and the Cheetah Conservation Fund in Namibia, we have a much clearer picture of what ails the cheetah today. Loss of habitat and its natural prey, conflict with livestock owners and illegal trade are the main causes of the decline, with cheetahs now confined to less than 10 per cent of their historic range. There are perhaps as few as seven thousand left in the wild, prompting renewed calls for the cheetah to be upgraded from Vulnerable to Endangered on the IUCN Red List. Ironically, national parks and game reserves set aside to protect all wildlife often harbour high densities of those same lions, hyenas and leopards that impact most strongly on cheetahs. Not surprisingly, perhaps, more than 65 per cent of wild cheetahs are to be found outside protected areas, where numbers of these competing larger carnivores are generally lower, but where fragmentation of habitat, loss of natural prey and conflict with livestock owners are greatest. It is very apparent that solutions to the plight of the cheetah must embrace ways in which local communities and big cats can live together in these unprotected lands.

With illegal trade in elephant and rhino 'products' dominating the headlines, the trade in live cheetahs seems to have slipped under the radar. It is only recently that the general public has been alerted to the scandalous and illegal trade in cheetah cubs to the Middle East, where they are prized as exotic pets. Typically cubs are captured in East Africa and shipped to the Yemen for onward travel. Less than 50 per cent of the cubs survive the journey. With all this to contend with, the cheetah needs all the friends it can muster in its race for survival.

There can be few more passionate or dedicated supporters of the cheetah than Her Royal Highness Princess Michael of Kent. She is the Royal Patron of both the Hoedspruit Endangered Species Centre in South Africa, which works to conserve vulnerable species and breeds cheetahs with a view to releasing them into the wild, and also of the Cheetah Conservation Fund in Namibia, which addresses threats facing the cheetah. In fact, the Princess loves cats in all their many different guises, both large and small. Sublimely beautiful Burmese and Siamese cats stalk the rooms at Kensington Palace, purring loudly with contentment as they slip from one lap to another. But as you will read in this fascinating account of Princess Michael's life in Africa as a teenager, big cats are not pets and their natural home is the open savannah. When she was given an orphaned cheetah cub to raise, she was always intent on returning it to the wild.

The Princess's tale is told with a refreshing candour; she says what she feels. You can almost smell the heady aroma of wild Africa, feel the joy of days on safari deep in the jungles of Mozambique on the sprawling farm where she came to know her father and stepmother. Her experiences fuelled her deep commitment to the world's wild creatures and their dwindling natural landscape, not least Africa's iconic big cats. Half a century on, the cheetah still holds a particularly special place in her heart.

AUTHOR'S NOTE

Although I have written three history books and three historical novels, I confess I never had it in mind to write *A Cheetah's Tale*, primarily because I have never had any desire to write an autobiography. I felt this was a very personal story which happened at a difficult time both for my family relationships and, in terms of political change, for the country where the events took place.

Some twenty-five years ago, Mozambique, the setting of this story, emerged from a long and destructive civil war. My father's farm there, first known to me in the early 1960s when I was seventeen, was situated not far from the vast Gorongosa National Park, stocked with every species of African wildlife. After the war ended, the local people, who had endured a brutal sixteen years of conflict, were aware how much the animals in their territory had also suffered: hunted by both sides for bush meat and trophies, they had been effectively wiped out. People were also aware of the heroic efforts made by a few concerned conservationists since the war's end in 1992 to re-establish Gorongosa's wildlife population.

For some years I have been the Royal Patron of the Hoedspruit Endangered Species Centre (HESC) at Kapama in northern South Africa, which breeds cheetahs for release into the wild. At a result, I heard about and finally met the remarkable American conservationist Greg Carr, who, since 2004, has made it his life's work to restore and restock Gorongosa to its pre-civil war splendour.

Apart from the herbivores, which have returned naturally to the security and good grazing in the park, Greg has reintroduced elephants, lions and leopards. I was so enthused by his efforts that a dream formed in my mind: to reintroduce cheetahs into Gorongosa, cheetahs from Kapama. Forty-three years ago I had released my own hand-reared cheetah into Gorongosa. I know she survived and bred, but after that I no longer kept in touch – I wanted her to be truly wild. By re-establishing a colony of cheetahs in Gorongosa, now when there were none left, I would be able to 'close my circle'.

For a long time I have been aware of cheetah populations diminishing due to loss of habitat, poaching and the capture of cubs for the illegal pet trade that so distresses me. But it was because of this personal connection and in the hope that exposure might help to end the trade in baby cheetahs, that I finally decided to write about my youthful experiences.

Sadly, I have no photographs from that period. During Mozambique's long civil war, my father's farm, like so many others, was ransacked. Among the general destruction, our books were taken from the library, piled up as a pyramid in front of the house and set alight. Among them were the family's precious photograph albums – mine included. All were destroyed. That loss hurts the most. They held my memories of an enchanted time spent in a world now lost.

As a result of my work in conservation, which I have espoused ever since, and my role as the Royal Patron of both the HESC and of the Cheetah Conservation Fund (CCF) in Namibia, I am kept well informed about the cheetah's delicate status. I am not an authority, but I listen and learn and remain an enthusiastic, active and supportive participant in a complicated world, helpfully advised by my friends in that field. By telling my story of a time spent with cheetahs, my hope is to draw attention to the predicament facing the world's fastest mammal – and perhaps help to save some space for this elegant, extraordinary animal in its natural environment.

'Surely the rights of people come before those of animals?' is the question conservationists are most frequently asked. And of course there can be only one answer. But I hope that the story I am about to relate will encourage some people to remember that animals have needs as well.

INTRODUCTION

I met my first cheetah when I was seventeen and visiting my father's farm in Africa for the first time. My parents had parted when I was an infant and my father had moved to Portuguese East Africa (Mozambique), started farming there and remarried.

I had not been long on Maforga, as the farm was known, before a local chief, whose village was on our land, came to ask my father if he would shoot a big cat which, he claimed, had taken a child from a hut. The animal had a damaged hind leg – caught in a trap – and could no longer hunt. My father had recently shot a lioness to save my life; the story had spread and the chief had heard it. Would Papi, as I called him, now come to save the children of his village and shoot the beast that was terrifying his people? 'Poor damaged creature,' muttered my father. 'Of course it's hungry if it can't hunt for its food' – but he had to agree. Taking me with him as well as his two African house hunters, he waited by the edge of the village. When the poor animal appeared, he shot it, an emaciated female cheetah.

On examining the carcass, Papi noticed at once that the cheetah was lactating: she must have cubs. She was so thin her ribs showed – hard to imagine she was feeding young. It was only while searching for the supposed remains of the child in the animal's lair that our hunters found a single tiny cub, its eyes not yet open. My father promptly said he would take it – it would not survive long in the villagers' hands – and he put it in one of mine, where it fitted easily. Sad little orphan – its mother had torn and chewed her foot out of a trap, almost starved and finally been shot dead. Of course I would try to take care of it...

And that is how Vitesse, or Tess as she came to be known, arrived in my life.

CHAPTER I

My parents had separated when I was too young to remember my father well. After World War II, when the lands of his country-living past were located in Soviet-conquered territory, he had made his way to South Africa, where he had friends. There was the prospect of big game to hunt (he was a famous shot and hunter) and he planned to examine some land he had somehow acquired in Portuguese East Africa, perhaps with a view to farming there.

By the time we met he was in his late sixties, still energetic and had not lost his sense of adventure nor humour. His Bavarian wife Rosemarie, who was fifty-four, had been a close friend of Karen Blixen, legendary author of *Out of Africa* and other books. They had been neighbours in Kenya, where Rosemarie and her first husband had also tried to grow coffee on land that was too high for the crop to prosper. Some years later, Rosemarie had been widowed once again, this time in Mozambique, where her late husband's land adjoined my father's. They met, married and began to cultivate a variety of crops, predominantly maize and citrus.

It had been agreed between my parents that I would visit my father for a long stay once I had finished school. I believe my mother was anxious that, if I went sooner, I might be seduced by Africa and not return.

Once I came to know something of the magic of that continent and my father's life there, I understood how right my mother had been. The exotic prospect of visiting my unknown, heroic-by-reputation and therefore idolised father in the jungle coloured my teenage years. I began to read all I could find about Africa, mostly about the animals, people and vegetation – at this time I had no interest in politics. I scoured a huge library of *National Geographic* magazines at a friend's house and, like most children, I cut out pictures and pasted them into scrap books. I read anything and everything I could find and probably fancied myself as some kind of Tarzan's Jane.

I had another reason which had piqued my interest. One day when I was about twelve and our class project was India, I had gone with my school on a visit to a museum. As I was looking at miniature paintings of sixteenth-century Mughals hunting, I was surprised to see what appeared to be a dog sitting behind a warrior on his saddle. What an extraordinary idea – to ride with a dog on the back of the saddle. Surely they ran alongside? Examining it more closely I saw that the animal wasn't a dog but a spotted cat. I thought it was a leopard. Or was it? I asked, and was told it was a cheetah, a big cat like a leopard, but taller and much lighter in body mass and bone.

These Mughals hunted with a cheetah sitting behind them on the horse? Amazing! I saw that their saddles were quite a different shape from ours and included a small platform behind. I was a passionate and accomplished young rider – in fact, I believed I could ride any horse – but with a cheetah sitting behind me??? I received strange looks from my teacher and the other girls when I fantasised about doing the same. Of course it was an impossible idea, but I would never forget that day and I believe it began my lifelong fascination with these alluring animals. Now I had a real project – find out about cheetahs for the day when I might see them in the wild.

Throughout my childhood, I would write to my father often, pestering him with questions about his life in Africa, and especially about cheetahs. Given that he lived there, I reasoned it followed that he would know the answers. It cannot have been much fun corresponding with a child forever asking questions, and he did his best. So did I – showing off what I had discovered. I kept all his letters and many years later, after his death, I found, to my surprise, that he had kept mine. There they were – a box full of them. And as I put our correspondence together, an entire picture of my feline-impassioned girlhood emerged.

Of course he did not know much about cheetahs – how could he? He was not interested in hunting them, and they were not really at home in the sort of subtropical jungle that surrounded his farm, preferring more open savannah. It was only through this collection of the letters we exchanged during my youth that I discovered he had written to everyone he could think of to give him the answers I craved. Having come to know him by that time, I realised this was not just to enlighten me, but also to have me think of him in the most favourable light, which of course it did. Papi adored women, wooed them assiduously, mostly for friendship's sake, and I was another he planned to conquer with his great charm. If it was knowledge about cheetahs I craved, then he, the consummate *chevalier*, would supply it.

Did I know, he once wrote, that the cheetah was the most primitive form of cat, having evolved some five and a half million years ago? He scored there – no, I did not, but I knew it had a dog-like muzzle and that unlike other big cats it hunted mostly by day, preferably in the early morning and late afternoon. I had seen pictures of leopards in trees with paws and tail hanging down, head resting on a branch – could cheetahs do the same? 'Do cheetahs siesta?' I asked in one letter. 'Yes,' he almost growled on the page back at me, '*I siesta too and NB will not be disturbed when I do.*' Humans and animals in Africa took a rest in the heat of the middle of the day – I got the message.

I spent contented hours in libraries researching the worldwide habitat of the cheetah, so much bigger in the past than it is today – all over northern Asia, Afghanistan, Africa and Persia (now Iran). Where are they now? The North Asian cheetah (recognised as a subspecies, *Acinonyx jubatus venaticus*) is virtually extinct; it survives in a few remote areas of Iran – well protected and kept under the watchful eye of the dedicated Mourad Tabhaz, who has been most helpful to me with information about them. But I doubt there are any left in its native Afghanistan. In Russia cheetahs died out due to the lack of their almost exclusive prey – goitered gazelle. Heavily hunted during the 1930s, the scarcity of these animals, and lack of alternative prey, led to the cheetah's extinction there.

As for cheetahs in India, there are none. A proud maharajah is photographed and on record as having shot the last three in 1947. When I read that the same man held the record for shooting 1,360 tigers, it made me want to weep with impotent rage. No doubt his overall cheetah bag was not worth counting.

Today there are only about 7,100 cheetahs in the wild, with another 1,700 or so living in some form of captivity. Namibia has the largest wild population, estimated to be some 1,500, and there is great agitation among conservationists in India about a controversial plan to import cheetahs from Namibia, reintroduce them and build up the population there once again.

It seems it has finally been decided that neither the lion nor the cheetah was indigenous to India. Most parties in the negotiations agree that since both species are said to have arrived with Alexander the Great in the fourth century BC, there can be no reason not to import them again! The fact that there is not enough suitable terrain for cheetahs in the parts of India where their food supply might exist seems of little consequence. Cheetahs need open territory and a plentiful supply of antelopes and other small animals they can hunt, since, unlike other predators, they require fresh meat every day. Of course the debate about the merits or lack of them with regard to indigenous and imported wildlife continues – and will continue, with typical Indian verbal circumlocution. But I did not know any of this at the time of my childish correspondence with my father.

Poor dear man – how I bothered him with a never-ending succession of letters. Since he had contributed little or nothing towards my upbringing and education, parental guilt sat heavily on the shoulders of this fearless warrior! He even persuaded my angelic stepmother to help him find answers to my stream of questions, writing letters on the ancient typewriter I came to know well, driving to the Post Office in the local small town to send them to potential big cat authorities within Africa, even around the world. It all must have become a rather tiresome labour of paternal love and I am sad I only knew and appreciated his gargantuan efforts much later. However, my passion for these elegant creatures did not abate, and once I had the responsibility of a cheetah cub I was glad to have my father's contacts with whom I could correspond on how best to raise it.

The thought of travelling to Africa if I studied well spurred me on to unimagined academic success. Just knowing that once I had finished school my mother would allow me to visit my father glued me to my books during term-time, while holidays passed mostly on horseback in a long daydream of Africa. I knew that Papi and Rosemarie spent some time away from the farm with friends on safari in the bush and that they each had a hunter's licence, without which one could not own a rifle in Portuguese East Africa. Much as I deplored the killing of any animal, I fully appreciated the need to hunt for food. But it was the animals I wanted to see. Papi had promised he would take me on a sight-seeing safari and show me everything.

I landed in Johannesburg in early October 1961 and was immediately enveloped in my father's great bear hug. He scooped me up and took me to the large house of friends, where I was made comfortable – spoiled, in fact. After a shopping spree, mostly for clothes that were quite inappropriate for my planned lengthy stay in subtropical Mozambique, we began the long drive north.

Papi's stop in Johannesburg had not only been to meet his beloved unknown daughter, but more importantly to collect a new Land Rover and a pedigree boxer puppy, which he gave me. Not the cat large or small I longed for, but something *to give me a sense of responsibility*, he said. I named her Calypso and adored her instantly. It was a nice touch and, as intended, it made me feel cherished and valued from the outset.

Meeting my father – in essence for the first time – was quite daunting. He was overwhelming in every way: tall and strongly built, with light skin and piercing blue eyes, though little remained of his platinum blond, straight hair; a fine-looking man with an impressive profile and strong personality. He turned the full force of his charm on me and I was easily won over.

I quickly discovered that he was also a great raconteur: on that long drive north he told me fabulous stories of his life in Africa and all the pleasures this Garden of Eden would provide for me. He had met a number of legendary figures and told me their stories, too. Robert Ruark was one I will never forget because

I met him later that year, another larger-than-life character who told tall tales around the campfire – or perhaps they were true: I could never be sure. He had published a book called *Uhuru* that year, a sequel to his earlier *Something of Value*, neither of which I had as yet read. Listening to him talk about it in his deep husky voice made an enduring impression on me, even more so once I had read the books. *Uhuru* means 'freedom' in Swahili and both books dealt with the Mau-Mau uprising in Kenya and that country's bid for independence. The racial bias and political aspects rather passed me by at the time; it was his writing about the countryside – jungle, savannah, the animals – that gripped me, as well as his mesmerising hunting descriptions: we were a wildlife-obsessed family, after all.

Only later, when I came to travel within Africa, did I begin to understand the many causes of the racial tensions of the time, and of the fight for independence. When I visited Kenya, some years later, it struck me that such a beautiful place could quite easily have been the site of the biblical Garden of Eden. Today, there are times when, reading the news, I imagine the snake is on the loose there again, offering an apple...

An eternal positive thinker, my father made no mention of the downside to the Paradise he described to me so eloquently – the venomous snakes, the mosquitoes which carry all sorts of illnesses, deadly spiders, scorpions, huge rats and other such domestic creatures. Fortunately I had been well prepared: *Never put on a shoe without shaking it out first; never go to the bathroom at night without a torch or candle, there may be a snake cooling itself there* and so on. But even this had failed to disenchant me – I was too excited from the build-up of many years' fantasising.

On that drive from Johannesburg, I listened to my father's unlimited supply of wild animal stories, each more thrilling than the last. I watched the landscape changing from dark green jungle to savannah and desert, flat and then mountainous and green again. I saw much game and heard all about it, too – the different types of zebra and giraffe, the many kinds of monkeys and baboons, their breeding habits and much more. We had two stops for the night at the comfortable houses of friends, before arriving at the South African/Rhodesian (Zimbabwean) border. I was quite tired and held my puppy Calypso sleeping on my lap. My father laid a shawl over us both, indicating I too should sleep and say nothing if approached, while he went into the Customs shed with my passport. Two men came out, but I remained with my head resting against the back of the seat, eyes closed. I heard my father telling them I was car sick and, seeing that mine was the pale face on the passport, they let me be. Once we were on our way, Papi told me that one normally has to get out of the vehicle at Customs, but since I was smuggling a puppy I had to stay still. *Smuggling a puppy?* 'Oh yes, you could have gone to jail,' he chuckled. Maybe he was right, but I was never quite sure about anything he told me after that.

Since it was a very long drive and knowing of my passion for the cheetah, sweetly he had prepared to entertain me by telling me stories about them. Did I know that the cheetah had been handled in captivity for over five thousand years? That the name 'cheetah' derives from the Hindi *chita* or 'spotted one' – or perhaps even earlier from the Sanskrit word *chitraka,* meaning 'speckled'? So my father was an expert on cheetahs after all? 'No, dear girl,' he wasn't, he told me, but as far as I was concerned, he put up a pretty good show.

I was curious – 'Can they swim?' I asked. I had seen a film where tigers did.

'Well, they've been known to swim but they don't like it, in fact they don't even like getting the pads of their paws wet. A tiger will swim and lions have been known to get into water after prey they have attacked and which has taken refuge in a river or a lake. But even stranger,' he said, turning, 'of all the large cats, the cheetah is the only one that cannot roar. Their throats do not have the necessary floating hyoid bone.' I was not prepared to go into this − it was enough of a surprise to learn that my deified feline was known technically as a 'lesser cat' for that reason. Had I heard their unique vocalisation, perhaps at a zoo? No, I had not and this was news to me as well. He beamed.

Realising he was growing in stature in my teenage mind, Papi went on and trotted out more information, while I wrote down as much as I could in one of the little notebooks I would always carry and still do to this day.

'They were first tamed by the Sumerians, you know,' he said, with a sidelong look at me − after all, he had no idea how much homework I had done, but he knew I had studied Ancient History at school.

'Who were they?'

'Ah, so there is something you don't know!' he mused as I blushed. 'They were an early civilisation from around 4000BC who existed in the vicinity of the Fertile Crescent, that land between the Tigris and Euphrates rivers in Iraq. Have you heard of that?'

I nodded. 'Mesopotamia.'

'Well, around 4000BC there was a lot of trading going on in the region and by then the people had the wheel.' Silence from me. 'And the potter's wheel.' Silence again. 'And they made and decorated pottery they fired in kilns. The Sumerians were the first people to write – they used clay tablets which you can see in museums today,' he said proudly, correctly reading my silence as ignorance. He scored again. I sensed this would become a competition. Leo and Capricorn – not signs that went well together. He was the lion – I, the goat, might well be eaten…

But I was becoming suspicious. 'Papi, how do you know all this? Mami said you didn't have the classical education that she had and that she pushed us towards; that you went to military school and that you were a well-known shot and hunter; that you farmed and bred horses when you were young; and that all you could talk to me about was crops, horses and European wildlife.'

He clammed up.

After some ten silent minutes: 'One can go on learning all one's life, you know, my darling daughter.' Did I hear a hint of petulance?

'Well, I thought it was the Egyptians, the Pharaohs, who trapped wild cheetahs and tamed them as pets?'

'And they did, but first came the Sumerians.' So I wrote it down – and I would check.

'Mami said you had an *Encyclopaedia Britannica* at the farm. Is that true?' It was. Considering we were speaking in German, I was surprised when he told me that Rosemarie had brought it with her from Kenya. She had kept it stored in Nairobi, where she had lived with her first husband, and when she was settled in Mozambique, she had sent for it. *Yes, she will be my friend, if she has an* Encyclopaedia Britannica *in the African bushland, where they don't even have electricity or a telephone.* I felt myself warming to my unknown stepmother even more than from gratitude for all the photographs of wildlife and their histories she had been sending me over the years; pictures that always had *her* handwriting on the back even if they were sent by my father.

For a while, Papi had satisfied my curiosity with his stories, and I sat in silence, absorbing the unfamiliar vegetation and scenery, cuddling the puppy and daydreaming contentedly. He too seemed lost in his thoughts – perhaps his interest in me had waned, at least for the time being. My father was much older than my mother; born at the end of the nineteenth century, at sixty-eight he was more the generation of a grandparent, and I had been warned that he still believed 'children should be seen and not heard'. He had fought as a cavalry officer in World War I, 'on a horse with a sword', he told me, although of course he also had a rifle. He had been severely wounded, decorated and spent most of the war in hospital. As a result, he limped a little, and elegantly, for ever after. On the one hand he was full of charm and bonhomie, but on the other he was something of a stern grandfather. Perhaps I had begun badly; been too cocky and all-knowing...

After some time, I tried again, tentatively, 'Dearest Papi, won't you tell me about the Pharaohs and their relationship with cheetahs – you seem to know so much.' I said this as winningly as I could. Little did I know then that he had recently acquired all this knowledge in a concerted effort to impress his daughter – and perhaps even keep me in Africa! Later he would often say, 'Your mother has had you for seventeen years, now it's my turn,' but I don't believe he really meant it. *Better seen now and then only, and definitely not heard...*

'Ah, yes, the Pharaohs,' he muttered, as if searching the filing cabinet of his prodigious memory, 'you must talk to Rosemarie – she knows more about them.' And that made me realise he did not really know all that much. Getting to know one's father at seventeen was difficult – I was almost grown-up and in another age I could already have been married with children. For the moment I decided it was better for me to rearrange the puppy and sleep for a while.

When I woke we were climbing and turning on the twisting road heading up to Umtali (now Mutare) and Papi told me we were almost at 1,200 metres: 'Even in the hottest months we can come here and be cool – we often do,' he said. It was a heavenly place, lush green foliage all around and in the valleys below, with the Vumba mountains massif to the southeast. 'Vumba means mist in the local tongue,' Papi told me, 'and in the mornings this valley is shrouded and cool during the summer months. That's when we usually come here; and to see the birds, which are exceptional. Are you interested in birds?' Not really, I told him – but regretted it later when I tried to make up for it. 'Ah, well, the leopards then.' Silence. 'You mean there are leopards up here?' Silence. 'Yes, my darling, and on the farm as well!' More excitement awaited me.

We stopped, let Calypso out and I breathed in deeply the delicious air – and the view. All around me, everywhere I looked, the world was dusted in a soft shade of mauve. 'Jacaranda time – October,' was all Papi said, smiling. I had never seen anything as beautiful. We drove on slowly down a street lined on either side with these trees and when we turned we found ourselves in a high tunnel made by the branches reaching across the street and joining high over our heads, the bluish-mauve flowers dangling from the boughs above us. It was as if we were seeing the world through a mauve-tinted telescope, everything covered in jacaranda flowers, from the ceiling of our tunnel to the carpet of blossom beneath our wheels. There were few cars then and the flowers lay deep without having been churned up by traffic. We stopped for a meal at a roadside café and admired the view to the Vumba mountains from this true corner of Paradise – our jacaranda heaven.

From Umtali we wound our way down to the valley border point where we would cross into Mozambique. I would make this crossing often thereafter and it never ceased to give me the same thrill, twisting up into the heights of Umtali, though never again at jacaranda time. Later, when we visited the town during the summer to enjoy its cool morning mists, the world around me had turned a brilliant red, pink and even some yellow. This complete change of spectrum was due to the flowering 'flame' or 'flamboyant' trees, which grew as high as twelve metres and had an even wider spread. Situated among so much natural beauty, Umtali never lost its crown in my eyes, no matter what anyone told me.

'Am I smuggling Calypso again? Should I sleep?' I asked, but no, I was told, nobody would mind here (not in 1961, anyway). At the border I saw a number of Portuguese as well as Africans at the immigration booth, all signing their names with a thumbprint. Papi explained that they were labourers, there for a contracted number of years and working hard on the railways to send money home to their families in Portugal. That is how the agricultural produce of Mozambique (no minerals had been discovered at this time) was brought to the coast for export or sent on inland to South Africa and beyond. The roads were always full of pot-holes after the rains and never really maintained; the railway was the surest way for goods to travel safely.

A deep breath as we crossed into Mozambique: my new home – well, for a while. After a drive of about a hundred kilometres which took us over two hours through lush thick bush as well as grassland on either side of the road, we passed through Vila Pery (now Chimoio and quite large!). It was a pretty little Portuguese town and the home of our doctor and medical clinic, its few shops with loggias in front trailing purple, red and even pink bougainvillea. There were several scrappy dogs here and there, and children with bright eyes and wide grins waving to us. Then on for another twenty-five kilometres to our local village of Gondola. There we stopped briefly to collect the post and some provisions for the farm, and then, not more than ten minutes later, we turned off the main road.

To my surprise we drove immediately into dense vegetation, down a winding path through compact cool jungle forming a dark tunnel above us. Our headlights on, I saw a number of monkeys, some swinging through the trees as if to race our jeep, shrieking with displeasure at the intrusion or screaming with the laughter that always seemed to accompany them. Small antelopes appeared and disappeared again; a furry face with big eyes ringed with white fluff popped out, stared and vanished. There were birds calling and much small game – dik-dik and other little antelopes, a warthog with young ran along the path in front of us for a while, the piglets holding their tails up vertically; there were more monkeys swinging about and chattering, but I saw no larger animals. Sensing my disappointment, Papi turned and said that there were quite a lot hiding in the thick shrubbery; in the early days of his working to develop the farm they had even seen the occasional leopard. 'We lost one or two of our dogs to leopards. Oh, and the lions, you will hear them calling at night. They come quite close to the house.' Was he just trying to frighten me? The drive was certainly having its effect on Calypso, who could not keep still and barked at anything that moved around us.

After some ten minutes spent weaving slowly through this magical forest, long liana vines hanging down for the monkeys to swing on, we emerged into a large clearing – green lawns to right and left and in front as far as I could see; then we turned to the right and there was the house. A low, flat, thick-walled villa, rather like those I had seen driving north from South Africa – half hacienda, half mission, painted a honey cream. It seemed to be sitting firmly on the edge of an escarpment which sloped down into a deep valley that turned from shades of green to mauve and then to dark purple in the far distance. Lawns surrounded two sides of the house, with huge shrubs of flowering hibiscus planted into them almost at random. There were tall moonflower trees (not the little shrubs of suburban gardens) with pink, white and pale yellow trumpets in flower, their heady afternoon scent mingling with that of the pungent white tobacco plants lining the drive and wafting through our open windows even before we arrived. Here and there, deep red bougainvillea climbed aimlessly up trees and lay flat on their tops, like washing drying in the sun.

Some weeks later, I flew with Papi over the farm in a friend's small plane, a Piper Comanche that had seen better days. It had a passenger door that would fly open flat back against the fuselage, forcing me to reach all the way out to retrieve it. From the air I saw that part of the farm was cultivated almost up to the road, but with a solid boundary 'wall' of trees three or four thick. Up to that tree line, dense foliage had been stripped and replaced by fruit trees and other crops. All that remained of the original jungle, after the land had been cleared to build the house and make the garden, was the strip about a kilometre wide leading from the main road. With the drive winding through it, we and any visitors could enjoy the illusion of arriving at civilisation through a dense wilderness.

And civilisation it was… Even before we stopped, I spotted tea elegantly laid on a table on the lawn, my eye caught by the egg-yolk yellow tea-set on a green tablecloth almost concealed within that sea of grass. As children, we used to play a game my mother said her mother had taught her – another way to keep us quiet, I think. Whenever we returned from an outing, we had to write a description of what we had seen or heard or make a drawing of the place or the people from memory. There were always prizes as an incentive.

In this way we learned to take in our surroundings, buildings, interiors, colours, faces, and to listen and recall conversation. I still write things down, not in a diary, more a journal of notes and descriptions, jotted into little pocket books, of places, objects, rooms, gardens, a hat passing by or dogs being walked, anything that catches my attention. Will it keep Alzheimer's at bay? I find myself constantly forgetting names. But I remember I noticed the yellow china tea service...

Calypso and I were instantly embraced by my stepmother Rosemarie, whom I came to love as if she were my own, one of the most special people in my life. She had been very beautiful as a girl and was still, I thought, although in her mid-fifties — old to my teenage mind. But an adult life spent living in Africa, no matter how much one tries, is not ideal for fair-skinned Europeans. I think she smeared zinc on my nose at that very first moment; perhaps it was only the next morning. Zinc was to accompany me everywhere I went thereafter, as well as a hat and a pair of khaki cotton gloves — with the fingers cut out — to protect my hands. Rosemarie promised I would thank her one day when, at her age, I would not have any brown spots on the backs of my hands. She knew.

Soon to be added to my daily uniform was a first-aid belt with every sort of medication I had to learn to use — but that would come later. I discovered that it was not considered decorous in a Portuguese colony for white women to leave any part of their bodies uncovered and I had to fight to be allowed short sleeves. I was given, and thereafter always wore when outside, long khaki trousers and shirts with sleeves rolled up, a hat against the sun and, during the day time, zinc on my nose.

Later, when I visited friends in Rhodesia for the weekend, I was rather surprised to see the daughters of the house wearing 'shortie' pyjamas and bikinis by their swimming pools, quite unconcerned about being exposed in front of the staff. That would simply never do across the border in Mozambique. Whereas I was welcome to stay with them, they were not very keen to visit me and be expected to cover up.

I met our dogs – four boxers wriggling with pleasure, bending like bananas from side to side the way they do, and five ridgebacks jumping up with joy at seeing my father – and I was instantly enchanted with my surroundings. The household had been lined up to greet me – 'Ba'as's daughter'. I heard their names and responsibilities in the traditional way of greeting, my hands clasped upright as if in prayer were then folded briefly between theirs as they bent their heads a little over them, bowing. Papi had told me that the local people were from the Shona tribe, which had a number of branches, and I determined to learn some of their language so that I could communicate without having to learn the local Portuguese dialect. In fact, I was not permitted to learn the Portuguese spoken locally – on my father's strict instructions; he would be ashamed, he told me, if I spoke the Mozambique dialect when visiting friends in Portugal and his daughter were thought to be an uneducated peasant! He may well have been right. Years later visiting Lisbon I did try some words and met with very odd looks.

Some of the staff had unlikely names in a Portuguese colony: there was Schultz, who looked after my father's clothes ('and always steals my white boxer shorts! He says they are so nice, why not? And he wears them with pride on *top* of his khaki working shorts – no concept of *under*wear!'). I quickly realised that the principle of 'mine' was also 'theirs'. Antonio the cook – 'his speciality is any game meat'; Wute Facenda – a name he had taken from a poster advertising some form of tax collecting, he claimed – he was Papi's cook on safari. Most important, I met Ravo, our *capitano*, who was

in charge of all and any hunting. There were a number of others –
but no female staff in the house, though there were several busy in
the outside kitchen and laundry.

I was given my own houseboy, Francisco, aged about fourteen,
without whom I was never to go anywhere, even into the garden
– 'snakes', I was told, and everyone nodded, rolling their eyes.
He carried a large panga, a wide, curved chopping sword. 'Good for
cutting, memsahib, grass or weeds or – heads off!' and he shrieked
and giggled like a girl, bent double, slapping his thigh. Francisco was
a strikingly handsome lad, with thick curling lashes and a brilliant
smile. 'Half Masai,' Papi said, 'speaks English. I brought him from
Rhodesia to look after you,' which was good to know, since I knew
not a word of any of the local languages. Of course it had been
Rosemarie's idea to borrow him from friends in exchange for one
of her houseboys whom she wanted to learn English.

In the late afternoon sunshine, the house glowed a soft
primrose, the roof a deep red. Built on a raised floor about sixty
centimetres off the ground, it had four wide, shallow steps leading
up on to an even wider terrace and the double entrance door.
Ingenious trellising covered in plants concealed the gap between
the house and the ground. The front faced the manicured lawns
and on the left, if one stood facing the entrance, the terrace
continued for some ten metres before bending sharply at right
angles down the length of the long house. I walked up the steps,
and on to where the terrace turned and caught my breath.
The ground dropped away sharply below the balcony, down a
long valley and towards the coastal city of Beira, lost in the haze
and too far away to see.

As I entered the house, the first thing I noticed was large areas of
shining deep-red floor, somehow looking cool on a hot afternoon

and gleaming blood red, which is what I discovered it was – animal blood mixed into the concrete and then heavily waxed to a glassy finish. Colourful kilim rugs were scattered here and there between deep old-fashioned sofas and armchairs loose-covered in floral linen. Papi's ancestors graced the walls – not very good paintings, I thought, but perhaps it was just as well in that damp climate. Taken to my room, I sighed with contentment. The walls were lined in dried, fine, honey-coloured grasses – 'to absorb the humidity'. Large, wide, shuttered windows faced the driveway and front lawns. Framed in the one opposite my bed I could see, far in the distance, a small mountain called something like Nyara Nyara, a perfect pyramid, as if drawn by a child on a postcard.

Papi had told me that when he first arrived in Mozambique to look at his land, he had found only jungle – no house, nothing cleared, just a storage building containing camping equipment and wonderful old tents which divided into rooms, something never seen in those days in Africa. These were permanently stored for the family to use and for friends who would visit to join them on safari.

Initially, Papi had wanted to build on his land and, ever practical, had climbed tall trees to seek out the best views. But Rosemarie loved the house she had lived in for some years so much that when they married they decided to stay there and not build anew. That was the house I had come to. The deep terrace ran around three sides of it, the fourth incorporating the pantry and facing the kitchen yard – chickens and turkeys running about – with the cookhouse on the other side of it. No smell of cooking was to enter the main house! Later I was amazed to discover that most of the cooking was done with the pots sitting on three round stones over a fire in their middle. From this most basic of kitchens emerged gastronomic delights I can still recall with pleasure.

All the windows were built wide to enjoy the views, but with shutters to shield against the bright light, despite the shade cast by the roof over the deep terrace. The shutters were useful during the monsoon season, too, when rain would lash out horizontally. Looking into the house from the entrance steps, I could see one room leading into the next, a long enfilade of large spaces all facing that glorious vista towards the coast – at first a rich green, then slowly turning darker into an indeterminate dusky grey and finally indigo, all the way to the sea in the far distance.

We spent many evenings sitting on the terrace talking, mesmerised by the headlights of the few cars slowly winding their way home from the coast. Although it was only 170 kilometres away, the drive could take close to three hours, especially if flooding had washed away the bitumen from the road, which seemed to be the case in most years. The pot-holes were (and still are, I am told) big enough to swallow a small car! And in those days the bitumen formed a single lane down the built-up centre of the road, which meant swerving off and down into the sloping red-clay gutter to avoid oncoming traffic.

When I arrived in the early 1960s, the area around the farm was infested with tsetse flies, and no domestic cattle could survive there. At least once a month, we would drive to Umtali and, while Rosemarie visited the hairdresser, Papi and I shopped for milk, spare parts for farm equipment (mostly British) and some domestic meat wrapped with ice in dish cloths and tied up tightly in newspaper. How easy it is to forget the days before picnic cooling boxes.

For our daily needs, we used powdered milk or Carnation in our tea or coffee, and when we brought back milk from Umtali, we often made our own 'fat milk' – a sort of junket. A bowl of milk would be left standing in the pantry, covered against flies but in the warmth until the milk 'turned', when it was put back into the refrigerator in its bowl. For a delicious dessert, we would add cinnamon and sugar or homemade jam. We had fresh baked bread every day and other homemade luxuries such as soap made from our own avocados, themselves a substantial export.

Papi told me of the effort he had originally made to ensure they had fresh milk for the house. A sad little Jersey cow was shut in a barn with wire netting over windows and doors to keep her safe from the tsetse flies. The poor little thing had a miserable existence, never going outside, but she was brought fresh grass. Then one day, a zebra died giving birth to twins – most unusual for zebras, I was told. The foals needed milk and the local vet, knowing Rosemarie had a cow, brought them to her. Precautions were taken so that the cow could not kick the young zebras. And they thrived! Rosemarie adored them, called them Hanzel and Gretl, and they followed her like dogs. She was determined to train them to pull a pony cart and had a plan to drive them into the little local town for her shopping and the post. What stories she told me of how they fought and bit and kicked one another in that little cart – although they were very friendly towards each other when out of the harness – and how often they managed to turn it over! Luckily she was never hurt, but flowers and gardening equipment would fly out, as well as a dog or two, who viewed Hanzel and Gretl with great suspicion thereafter. Finally Papi had enough – the carpenter spent all his time repairing the pony trap and the zebras were getting worse not better, living up to their fairy-tale names. He insisted, and a reluctant Rosemarie – who had never, ever failed to tame an animal – had to agree to let them be given to a nature reserve.

Our shopping trips to Umtali focused mainly on our need for repairs and spare parts for farm vehicles. For some reason everything on the farm with an engine broke down, to a litany of

Papi's resounding curses. Since our only source of energy came from giant gas canisters, or the batteries removed from our vehicles, we did not have sufficient power to use electrical tools to make repairs, and somehow my father never found a good handyman among his workforce. I think mechanical breakdowns were the greatest cause of his irate explosions.

Umtali was also a source of things I yearned for – magazines, library books in English (something Rosemarie had arranged for me) and, not least, cigarettes! Neither Papi nor Rosemarie smoked, but Rhodesian tobacco was famously delicious and cheap. The flat packs were rectangular, the size of a shallow book, two cigarettes deep. Called First Lord, they looked supremely elegant in their white packs edged in dark blue and gold. Naturally I began smoking...

Aside from the domestic meat we collected from the butcher in Umtali every month or so, the alternative was wild game and Papi employed two licensed hunters, Assia and Rodrigo, overseen by Ravo the *capitano*, to shoot for the pot. Since only about a quarter of the farm, around eight hundred hectares, was under cultivation, there was much jungle between and around it that teemed with small game. Assia and Rodrigo reliably succeeded in bringing us a variety of small antelopes or a baby bushpig, but one of my favourites was guinea fowl: slow, heavy birds prone to sitting together on the low branches of trees in their feather coats of tiny white spots on grey. They never sat in trees elsewhere that I had seen them, but at the farm I think they hoped to escape the attention of the dogs!

There were some birds that liked the fruit of the few pawpaw trees planted on the outer edge of the lawn and they attacked it mercilessly. I suggested netting the fruits, but Papi said, 'Leave them be. After they have eaten, wait a few days and when they return, and they will, *then* we can shoot them. The fruit will make their liver taste delicious.' Not foie gras, I grant you, but making something delectable with what one had available in the bush was always a challenge.

Some chickens and turkeys, destined for the table, were kept firmly in the area between the house and the kitchen hut, and behind high wire netting. For festive occasions, and especially at Christmas time, the chosen turkey would receive a treat. Gently though firmly wedged between a pair of knees, it was given a generous swig of brandy and then allowed to go free. I swear that turkey would chuckle as it walked about rather unsteadily, telling the other birds about its good luck. 'Rather like being offered a favourite last meal before your execution,' I suggested. Papi was not amused. 'The turkey is happy and the brandy makes it taste much better for us!' More culinary tricks of life in the bush! The poor turkey staggered about like a tipsy old lady before meeting its end on the chopping block. The cook swore by the system, but I am not so sure: with no other domestic meat available, I suppose the hausfrau must be inventive...

For permission to hunt in this Portuguese colony, a licence was mandatory and taken very seriously by the authorities. Once such a licence was purchased, the holder had the right to shoot one elephant a year, two buffaloes and more of the lesser game. Papi assured me he was against shooting any wild cat, big or small. I am still not convinced that he did not adopt this rule for my sake – the news of my love of felines had long preceded my arrival. Although we ourselves never ate the meat of the elephants or buffaloes that were shot, our farm workers loved it, especially the liver, and the rest was cut into strips which they hung from high wooden racks over hot coals in an outside yard. The resulting biltong was cherished and chewed slowly for some time. In those days there was no shortage of big game and regrettably, in the early 1960s, we did not yet have conservation in mind. I have done my best throughout my adult life to compensate for that. The Africans' food was usually a sort of dried flaky fish brought in sacks from the coast. This was mixed with mealie maize, and the occasional change to buffalo or elephant biltong was much appreciated.

We had two categories of farm hands. The *contratos* or contract workers were employed through an agency for a specific length of time, usually two years, and were not locals. They would receive only a portion of their pay so that they did not drink it all on their day off. The balance would be sent to their families or given to their labour chief for safekeeping. At first, I could not understand how our workers were often drunk on their day off when they were forbidden to buy alcohol, a known weakness. It did not take me long to realise they could make their own by fermenting almost any fruit or vegetable grown on the farm.

The other category of workers were known as *voluntarios*. There were a number of little village settlements on the parts of our land we had not yet cultivated and, by law, each family had to send one male family member to give us a number of days' free labour to cover the amount of tax we had to pay if they lived on our land. I imagine the authorities assumed we would use them as slaves, and saw them as an 'asset' we had to pay for! We came to know a number of our *voluntarios* well, especially since their wives and children would come in the evenings to our little makeshift clinic. This had been set up by Rosemarie and was the custom amongst farmers throughout the country. In the beginning I was rather lonely on the farm – both Papi and Rosemarie had a lot to do and did not want me walking around outside on account of the snakes –

so I was happy to be involved with the clinic. My instructions were to search for lice in the children's hair and to dispense Aspirin for anything and everything mild. If someone was truly ill, they were taken to the clinic in Vila Pery – the nearest town of any size – the next day.

Working evenings in the clinic, I came to meet the wives of our *voluntarios,* whom one did not see very often. Some of them I found extraordinarily beautiful, but they married very young and produced children annually, so their beauty did not stay long. Papi told me it was a sign of my acceptance by them that they would bring their children to the evening clinic. After a while I would also spend one afternoon a week at the local mission school and teach a little English – not a great success – but we sang songs and I taught them German nursery rhymes, skating over some of the translations.

One evening a man from one of our villages was brought to the clinic with the most horrible, festering, large sores on one leg, almost exposing his bone in places. The story his companions related was that some days previously he had been asleep with his wife in their hut when a puff adder crawled in. In her sleep the wife had stretched out her arm, accidentally striking the snake, which bit her. The husband shouted, the snake was killed, its body thrown out behind the hut. The following day the wife died. But this happened during the puff adders' mating season and, according to the villagers, the dead snake's mate slithered into the hut looking for its partner – and bit the husband. His shouts alerted everyone, and the village witch doctor treated him with an antidote of his own making. True, the man had not died, but the result was this terrible rotting of his flesh and what could we do to help him?

Papi at once bundled him, still on his stretcher, into our open-backed Land Rover and, accompanied by several of the man's friends, drove fast to the clinic in town. That the poor man survived was the talk of all the workers for the next weeks and, although he had to lose his leg, he eventually came home quite the hero.

I have never been good about snakes (unlike my son and husband who do not mind them at all and have both worn pythons around their necks on occasion). Already on my first day at the farm I had been given a lesson in how to deal with snake bite from a doctor who came from the local clinic at my father's urging. Thereafter, I never left the house without wearing a belt containing all I would need in the event of snake bite – or without Francisco, my guardian houseboy, and his trusty panga. The sight – and the smell – of that poor man's leg did not leave me for a long time.

CHAPTER II

As well as the dogs around the house, there were a number of wild cats – the descendants of domestic cats gone feral. The dogs left them alone and they kept to the kitchen yard area of the house. They mostly spat, hissed and grabbed any scraps of food they could find, but we also fed them, since they took care of the rats, mice and even some small snakes. Given my enduring love of cats, it did not take me long to subdue some of them. The gas cylinders which powered the refrigerator made a warm spot in the cavity underneath; the cats often gave birth there and we left old blankets, water and food for them and the new mother. But no amount of nurturing stopped the kittens from spitting and scratching, and I wore thick gardening gloves until they resigned themselves to my caressing. Even before their eyes opened they would hiss and spit and later I learned from our local vet that this proved kittens possessed the sense of smell before sight.

Although Papi and I had travelled together all the way from Johannesburg, during that first week on the farm my darling sensitive stepmother was aware of the awkwardness that still existed between us. Her solution was that my father should take me on safari for a few days to their favourite place near Gorongosa National Park. Knowing how much he was in his element in the bush, with his great understanding of everything to do with animals and plants, trees and rivers, Rosemarie thought that spending time with him there would help me to get to know him better. That decided, she took me with her to the 'safari house', a concrete, windowless little building where the tents and everything else imaginable that might be needed for a comfortable stay in the bush were stored.

We had a merry morning sorting out what she thought I would appreciate for a few days alone with Papi – hammocks, shower equipment, Papi's specially made mahogany WC seat – not that there would be flushing water! The huge tents labelled for Papi, for

Rosemarie and for guests, the folding chairs, folding table, shooting sticks to perch on, parasols, dining equipment, turntable to attach to the Land Rover's battery (music was essential to happiness in the life of my family and still is), pressure lamps, washing bowls, mirrors for the canvas 'bathroom', trays, tablecloths, cutlery, china (!), *linen* napkins – I watched all this pile up and it seemed as if we were moving house, not spending a few nights in the bush.

Rosemarie was delighted at my wide-eyed astonishment and assured me I would be much happier with all the comforts she was providing. As I quickly learned and never forgot, she was always right.

Francisco was to come with us to look after me, as well as Papi's usual safari team, and although this was a viewing-only safari, we took Ravo along with us, 'just in case'. It was not quite the end of the hunting season, which ran from May to November. In fact, Papi wasn't quite honest with me about this: knowing that I wouldn't come on a shooting safari, he assured me the season was over. He was excited, he said, to show me the sights of this beautiful country without having to concern himself with his usual preoccupations when out hunting.

As well as Papi's guns, Rosemarie laid aside one of hers for me. Papi knew I could shoot – anyone taught by my Hungarian uncle (Papi's former brother-in-law) could shoot! My uncle had taken part in three Olympic Games for Austria and had been six times European skeet and clays champion. Not that I had any intention of shooting animals, but 'just in case', Papi repeated with a wink. I wasn't sure about the meaning of that wink and added it into my little journal that evening. Would we be in any danger?

With the Land Rover and two other vehicles packed with all our provisions and equipment, we set off amid waving and a certain amount of giggling from the gathered staff at the house. The sight of my mismatched safari get-up, a combination of small and slim Rosemarie's and large Papi's khaki clothing and his far too big pith helmet resting on my nose, had them all laughing merrily, as did the thought of Ba'as grinning optimistically at the prospect of being alone with his uninitiated daughter in the bush.

The only incident that occurred on the way was that we drove over a large snake on the main tarmac road. 'Mamba' was all Papi said, after he stopped and one of his men threw the body into the back of one of the vehicles. The weather was surprisingly good for the beginning of the rainy season, as was the road until we turned off into the bush. After about two more hours bumping across rough country we reached the chosen camping spot.

The concession my father used during the hunting season was situated south of a river called the Pungwe which formed the natural border of Gorongosa National Park, a wonderful area of over four thousand square kilometres of rainforest, savannah and grasslands, filled with all the wildlife one could imagine.[1] The moment we arrived I understood why this was my father's favourite campsite. Situated at the southern end of the Great Rift Valley, it had plenty of cover, a mix of tall and small trees typical of the local miombo woodland, and stretches of grassland beneath a high escarpment.

As I watched Papi's tent being erected, I was impressed – it looked most inviting. There was a sitting area left open as one entered with a folding canvas chair and a small table with a lamp; then a bedroom well sealed against any small wriggly intruder

---

[1] During the civil war in Mozambique, which lasted from 1977 to 1992, 90 per cent of the game was wiped out. Following the end of hostilities, private hunters came into the park and shot what was left.

and with two window openings, each covered by cotton mesh and topped with a rolled-up canvas cover to be let down for privacy or at night. There was a dressing area with a rail and shelving made from canvas stretched taut; pressure lamps stood on two folding camp tables, one in the dressing area and another next to the bed. This was large and looked comfortable and inviting. Yes, one such will do me nicely, I thought.

What I did not expect to hear was that my tent had been forgotten, left back at the farm! I swallowed my disappointment, not daring to ask where I was going to sleep. I need not have worried: in no time the trailer was fixed level, a large bag of straw covered in comfortable bedding put down as a mattress, sheets and blankets added, and a mosquito net hung from a tree over the four corners of the trailer that had now become my bed.

Bathroom facilities, too, were inventive and well served their purpose. First a semi-circular screen of tall dried grass was set up and within was placed a shiny mahogany seat for a WC. Fastened beneath the seat was a horseshoe-shaped metal ring from which several metal legs descended to an identical horseshoe-shaped ring. The seat-on-legs and matching base sat on the ground, the base with a gap in the front. This ingenious, strong and serviceable structure, designed by my father, was placed over a deep, narrow hole carefully dug, a hand shovel left lying tidily next to it on a small pile of soil. Around what could only be termed a throne, more dried grass was cut and laid on the ground as a covering. Hanging on a peg on the screen by one's left hand was a roll of loo paper on a string; on another peg on the right dangled a pair of binoculars. The entrance to the enclosure had a wooden half-door we had brought with us. In the morning I understood why. The whole construction had been strategically erected on the edge of the escarpment with a good view of the river below. According to Papi's philosophy of outdoor living, every aspect of safari life was to be savoured and there was much to enjoy looking through binoculars, either up at the birds in flight or down towards the trees and river below – not least the sight of crocodiles lolling about, idly waiting for a brave herbivore to leave the sanctuary of the park and cross over, tempted by the maize purposefully planted on the opposite bank.

As for washing, a shower was installed inside another semi-circular grass screen. There was a wooden rack to stand on and a large bucket hung overhead with a pulley which released the warm water just poured in. One pulled the cord to close the hatch and keep some water for the end rinse. The soap was our own avocado house brand, a miracle for the skin – and it hung in a net on a peg. By my trailer I had a washbasin for hands and teeth, even my own mirror. My initial disappointment about the tent forgotten, and otherwise satisfied with the domestic arrangements, Papi and I washed, changed into clean clothes and had a drink by the fire. Relaxed and in a loquacious mood, he told me stories until it was time for dinner.

Despite the surprising yet charming touch of tablecloth and candles – typical, I would learn, of Rosemarie who made everything attractive; even wild flowers had been picked from shrubs to decorate the table – our first safari dinner was not a success. The staff waited at table wearing white gloves, just as Karen Blixen's servants had been obliged to do on her safaris, which made their task of holding the slippery china plates almost comical (Why china on safari? I asked myself, but this was an older generation). Nonetheless, the stew looked and smelled promising and, with the addition of sweet-smelling wild herbs, tasted delicious. After dinner, I complimented Schultz, usually Papi's own servant but also his chef on safari, and asked him what was in it. He chuckled merrily: 'Mamba, missy.' It was the snake we had run over on the way to the camp. I rushed to the bushes – not a good start. Papi laughed as I weakly climbed up the huge tyre of the trailer and retired into the sanctuary of my mosquito-net tent, the temperature pleasant at least, the stars clearly visible above, and Africa's night calls loud around me.

Exhausted, I fell asleep, vaguely aware during the night of what I assumed was my father's dry coughing in the comfort of his splendid tent nearby. At dawn, I was startled awake by a loud bang, so loud it seemed almost in my ear. With knee-jerk reaction, I sat upright to see through my mosquito net my father in his pyjamas, crouched on one knee, his rifle at his shoulder and levelled in my direction. I looked down and saw a lioness lying dead alongside my trailer. It was she who had been 'coughing' all night (or 'wuffing', I heard it was called). Her paw prints were there on the top of the trailer's tyre and Papi said he had seen her when she had been on the point of springing up to eat me! In a daze, all I could do was reach for my simple box Brownie camera and take a picture of my father in that pose: on one knee, in pyjamas and his gun still levelled. It did look rather strange. Poor lioness. I could see she was no longer in her prime, quite thin and old, her coat flea bitten, and covered in scars even on her nose; I imagine I should have been easy prey. It was then that Papi told me he never shot big cats except when in danger. From the look in his eye I had the impression he almost regretted shooting this one – even to save me. I was sorry too, and naively asked why he had to kill it. 'So you think I should just have wounded it and then you could have played Florence Nightingale, healed her and let her go?' I realised this was silly, but...

It was during that 'bonding safari' that I saw my first big cat in the wild. I had heard many stories and seen pictures, but none compared with the majesty of a lion, leopard or cheetah in its natural surroundings.

Now that I was in the bush I kept a particularly close watch for the big cats and that same day I saw a leopard. The early morning sun glowed on his muscled, black-spotted tan body. He was halfway up a tall tree, jumping forwards in slow, controlled leaps, almost as if he were counting between each effort made, as he lifted up a much larger antelope in his powerful jaws. 'Pantry,' said my father, as I watched the leopard wedge the antelope between two high branches. 'I suppose you know that a cheetah will only eat fresh-killed meat, but leopards and lions will happily eat carrion, and this leopard will feast on its kill for some days.' (So cheetahs had to kill each day to eat… more pressure on them. Another note for my little book.) In the cooler afternoon we went out from the camp again, this time driving not walking, and Papi showed me herds of zebras, ostriches, wildebeest and buffaloes.

Supper was a cosy affair – a delicious saddle of antelope cooked on the open fire with wild herbs, local rice and red peppers. Then a cake we had brought with us to be eaten with sliced oranges. Papi was in full reminiscing mode and made me laugh often at his youthful adventures in the cavalry at the start of World War I. That night there was to be a full moon and, if we were fortunate, we might see buffaloes leaving the national park some distance below the escarpment to cross the Pungwe River and feed on the maize on the other side.

So much happens by full moon in Africa – or it has in my case, and this night was no exception. Even after all these years and many visits, I have never seen the moon larger, nor more orange, nor glowing more strongly than I have in Africa. As we sat and watched it rise, our binoculars trained on the river sparkling in the moon's reflected light, I saw the buffaloes, at least twenty of them, cross over slowly to feast on the maize, shaking their great heavy heads, mooing softly to one another, and the sound of their crunch-crunching on the maize husks rose up to our observation spot. Strange, the images that remain with one. I did not stay up to watch them slip back across the river.

The following morning, and the day after the drama of the lioness who had me on her menu, we rose early and drove across open country, watching the animals rising, the clear shape of where they had lain during the night still visible in the dew-covered grass. We had been driving for a couple of hours and seen much game, when I spied my first cheetah. We had stopped for morning tea on a termite mound, which are often as high as a small house, perhaps three or four metres, and can be very old. Cheetahs especially use them to study the landscape for potential prey, but this time we were the observers. We spread our tablecloth on the top and were unpacking our sandwiches and thermos of tea, when to my horror I saw ants appear from everywhere and crawl over everything. I looked at my father, who grinned, and I watched in awe as he picked up a sandwich covered in ants, bit and munched happily. 'Adds to the flavour – you'll see,' and I guess they did. Then he pointed and I lifted the binoculars hanging around my neck. There he was – in a large stretch of dry grass – my first cheetah about to make his charge. I zoomed in and watched open-mouthed as he ran, his action indescribably elegant, almost floating above the ground alongside his antelope target, whirling and twisting as he shadowed it, his long, white-tipped tail swinging to balance him as he made sharp turns. The antelope managed to escape, but that day I saw for the first time a cheetah at full speed hunting, and the thrill of it engulfed me. I had missed the stalk, but I felt confident there would be other opportunities.

To help me to really get the feel of the wild animals, Papi decided that we should drive into the national park itself, situated a little way on the other side of the river from our camp. It was the size of a small country and here, Papi promised me, I would be able to see the best of the local wildlife. We left at daybreak for our game drive there. As we drove down the escarpment towards the river, patches of fog drifted over the water; the sun was just rising, a beautiful morning as we headed for the pontoon bridge. Arriving at the river bank I recoiled at the sight of the many crocodiles, huge slugs the colour of the mud they lay in, eyes almost closed, malevolent. We drove over the bridge in the general direction of Chitengo, the park headquarters, then up the mountain road to Bue Maria, where we turned off to the right and into the park.

Already at the entry gate I was impressed by the smart way the formalities were conducted and the clear interest in conservation there. We drove in and stopped almost at once. Before us lay a wide, wide valley; on the horizon white clouds were lit by the sun, and all around us was forest – not more than five kilometres from the park entrance.

We drove a further eight or ten kilometres to the main camp where we checked into our bungalows. I noted they were clean and well kept – Rosemarie would ask me, I knew. As neither Papi nor Ravo was familiar with the roads in the park, we decided to take a guide.

We had hardly left the campsite when we saw game to the right and left of the road, mainly wildebeest, zebras and impalas, but also small gazelles. To my surprise, the impalas were reasonably tame and we were able to approach quite close. Papi said the reason was that inside the park they knew they were safe from hunters and I would be astonished how close we would be able to get to other animals as well. Wherever we looked there were enormous herds of every kind around us and the steppes were teeming with wildlife – an extraordinary sight to my novice eyes. But Papi said we had actually not seen much as yet.

'Look,' he said suddenly, and there stood my first buffalo. 'Now that's a big bull! Look at him!' he urged, his excitement palpable under his controlled exclamation.

Just then, the buffalo climbed out of his wallow, came towards us and stood about thirty metres from the jeep. He was a breathtaking sight, chewing slowly side to side and shaking his head, with several small birds – oxpeckers – sitting on his back, attending to ticks and the like. He stayed just long enough for me to take him in from top to toe before he moved slowly on his way.

We drove on, kilometre after kilometre through the Urema valley and its huge lake, the soul of Gorongosa, fed by three great rivers. We watched the herds of game there on the steppe of the Urema, which then flows into the Pungwe. Papi told me that these were really enormous marshes, great open stretches dotted with small ponds. And then he pointed out the varied birdlife – herons, eagles, vultures surrounding an old carcass. Never previously interested in birds, on that first safari I found the sight of them thrilling and became obsessed thereafter. There were Egyptian geese, wild ducks of all kinds, other geese, Goliath herons and many more I did not yet recognise, despite turning the pages of the bird book I had with me as quickly as I could.

Suddenly an elephant stood in front of us, quite close. He was not particularly big, but an imposing sight nonetheless. Papi looked surprised – and pleased at my enthusiasm. It must be infectious; I am his daughter, after all!

The road led to the so-called Paradiso – a name borrowed from the sixteenth-century Mughals in India, who used it to describe an enclosed hunting park, a place of privilege away from the people. The rulers kept these areas for their private pleasure of hunting and to help preserve their own mystique. In Gorongosa, the Paradiso was a raised concrete hide that gave visitors the chance to get out of their vehicles and observe wild game undisturbed and without risk; at ten metres above the ground, it was too high for any animal to reach.

This part of the park really deserved the name 'Paradiso'. In front of the hide we could see flooded parts of the plain fed by the Urema River, interspersed with marshes, a line of forest in the background. To the left open steppes were dotted with isolated palms, and an enormous quantity and variety of animals coming to the wet areas to drink. And such a diversity of migrating birdlife, Papi told me, as one can see only rarely: in addition to the ducks, geese and herons, I identified pelicans and storks – both the marabou and the European stork. A fish eagle flew over, winging away, and then suddenly it plunged into the water to emerge with a wild duck in its beak! I was spellbound.

I turned to see a pair of lions walking nonchalantly along, ignoring us, she leading with an elegant step in front of him, the Pasha, shaking an immense mane as he followed her. They came to drink, their mouths red with blood. 'Thirsty after feeding on their kill,' nodded Papi. Far in the background he pointed out seven big buffaloes which had also been drinking and were now heading back into the forest.

When it was time to move on, our guide advised we should go slowly because there were many elephants in the area; coming around a blind corner we could drive right into one. We turned the corner – and there they were. Five of them, including a big bull. We watched them cross the steppe in front of us, slow and solemn.

We drove on, and as the Land Rover stopped sharply on a bend, Papi said, 'On the left, now there's a really big one!' I looked and saw an elephant walking into a pond covered with water lilies. Totally indifferent to us, he just stood there, pulling up the plants with his enormous trunk, and began eating them. Papi remarked that it was the first time he had seen such a thing – and he had visited Gorongosa thirty or more times. Then I saw a hippo in the water, moving slowly towards the elephant, his head framed in water lilies just above the surface looking forwards. His ears were also turned forwards towards the elephant, as he moved very deliberately closer and closer, while the elephant calmly munched on, watching the hippo.

'Papi, what will happen now? Surely he doesn't mean to attack the elephant?' Just as I said that, the hippo submerged and disappeared. Another hippo began to move towards the elephant, again with just his head above water, and continued through the densely packed, bright blue-violet blossoming water lilies. It was a glorious tableau and Papi patted my knee, content at hearing my sigh of delight.

The elephant continued to stand there calmly chewing, barely noticing these 'small' visitors, enormous to my eyes. Frantically taking notes so as not to miss anything, I looked up to see a second elephant arrive and also enter the water for his morning bath. The same game was repeated: the hippos submerged and came closer and closer towards the elephant. 'What do they want?' I wondered aloud. 'Do they want to play with him? Or are they offended that the elephants have invaded their domain?' Papi just laughed. I found it all miraculously strange and wonderful without any idea of what was going on.

While we were still sitting there lost in the joys of nature, a third elephant arrived. 'Goodness, he's big,' I whispered to Papi in awe. 'And two buffaloes as well!' And all this was happening on the surface of quite a small pond, perhaps fifty to eighty metres wide and no more than a hundred metres long. My first sight of real Africa and it filled me with an overwhelming rush of pleasure to be sharing my father's wonderful world.

While we sat for at least another fifteen to twenty minutes to enjoy this picture, Papi told me he had never before seen anything like it, so many species of large game on such a small surface, nor the astonishing teasing games of the hippos with the elephants. I am only sorry I did not have my rather basic camera with me – stupidly I had forgotten it at the lodge. We had never been a photographic family and still are not. Perhaps that made me watch harder in order to remember and I continued to scribble in my notebook.

Just as we were about to drive on, two big elephants passed very close to our vehicle, fanning their great ears to and fro and hardly noticing us. Papi explained that, unlike what most people assume, this was a sign they are calm and not angry at all. 'If the elephant is angry he lays his ears forwards, raises his trunk and very soon after he has tested the wind he lowers his trunk like a periscope, pushes it out towards you and charges. When the elephant is peaceful and quiet, he fans his ears in and out, the trunk hangs down and he strolls along or stands there dozing.' So much to learn.

Seeing how keen I was to know more, Papi went on to explain that over his long life as a hunter he had found that the big old bulls were generally quite even-tempered, both in and outside the safety of the game reserves. 'If you don't come too close to them they won't bother you. It's quite a different story, however, with the old cows. Even when they seem to have worn away their tusks they can be extremely disagreeable. The local people here call them *maridi*; if a maridi pushes her ears forwards at you and starts to trumpet, best to get out of there as quickly as you can.' Although I took this advice to heart, when it actually happened to me, I failed to move – the famous day of my 'ossification' that was to happen a few months later.

We drove on and came upon a carcass we had noticed earlier and where now many vultures were quarrelling over the last remains of an animal killed by lions. 'Although vultures are a hideous species, their importance cannot be exaggerated; they are nature's health police,' Papi informed me cheerfully, full of satisfaction about our day and my initiation. He pointed to a marabou stork also feeding on the carcass, and an eagle sitting on a dead tree looking disdainfully down upon the low-life vultures.

The fish eagles in Gorongosa are a wonder to behold. Their heads and chests are white, their bellies a rich chestnut brown, the whole set off with black wing feathers – really beautiful creatures. 'To live,' explained Papi, 'of course they must kill. But isn't it marvellous to see an eagle circling in a blue sky? That miraculous, majestic movement as the great bird catches the air currents? That is really something special to see. When I hunted in the High Tatra mountains [now a part of Poland] and shot my great ibex, golden eagles circled over me. What a sight – the snow-covered mountains, chamois and ibexes below me in the valleys and, circling above me, golden eagles. Quite wonderful,' mused Papi, in love with nature.

I continued to ponder the logic of hunters – that to preserve one must kill, just like carnivores in nature. I knew that in his earlier years Papi had been in charge of all the hunting, shooting and fishing carried out in Silesia – now a part of Poland, an area the size of Scotland. Although I had always been averse to killing except for food, slowly over the next months I began to understand the need to kill in order to conserve – a great problem facing the world today. Indiscriminate killing does untold damage to a species, but careful decisions to match feeding areas to the number of animals, or game to their hunting areas, are what preserve wildlife. The hunter has always wanted to continue his sport for whatever reason – trophy or food – and, to ensure the supply continues, he must husband that supply. Whether for selfish or conservation motives, the same principle has applied to preserving wildlife – and has done so throughout time. It is wholesale slaughter, not careful husbandry, that is reducing precious animal populations.

The same morning our guide had told us that lions had killed a zebra quite early. From a distance we had seen the big maned lion lying by the carcass, roaring his pleasure at the success of his hunt. We decided to visit him once more. Papi spotted him first – 'Look, there he is, the "old gentleman", in the shade of an acacia' – and about thirty metres from him, we saw his consort and three full-grown cubs. Only the skeleton of the zebra remained.

As we drove several times round these lions, at a distance of twenty to thirty metres, we saw that they were not in the least disturbed by us; they did not even stand up to growl. They just lay there, sated, and observed us dully. Once I thought I saw a warning glance from the male when we came a bit too close, but I could have been wrong. On we drove, I thrilled to have witnessed this.

We continued to watch more game: waterbuck, even a herd of eland – the world's largest antelopes, huge, amazing beasts, with thick, twisting horns pointing backwards – standing not far from us, though they kept a wary distance since the lions were between us and them.

After such a glut of wildlife, Papi was still perturbed that there were two species he had not been able to show me: sable antelopes and kudus. He thought they might have gone up into the mountains, and there were no roads there. 'These noble antelopes mostly avoid places where other species gather. They're too proud to mingle with the ordinary folk,' and he laughed at my astonished look.

We saw impalas with their elegant movements, suddenly jumping high and playfully twisting about; then, just as unexpectedly, two bucks thrust at each other in mock combat. Sometimes the play turns serious – we saw two or three wounded impala bucks.

There was no end to the information which poured out of my father and I scribbled it down as quickly as I could. Something he told me struck me as surprising – how animals, including those from Gorongosa, behave quite differently as soon as they move outside the safety of the park: immediately they become exceptionally shy. And should a herd have been fired upon, you will not see them again, at least for some time: they will disappear back into the protected area. It seems animals know exactly where they are and become extraordinarily wary in the areas just outside a patrolled 'Paradiso'.

It was towards the end of that first remarkable day in Gorongosa that I saw two cheetahs hunting – two young brothers from the same litter, whispered our guide. I watched, hardly daring to breathe, as they slowly crept up towards their quarry from either side in the long grass, the one inching towards an antelope, driving it towards the other lying in wait, ready to spring. I saw how they both flattened their bodies and lowered their heads in the dry grass, completely camouflaged as they crept nearer. I continued to hold my breath as they edged closer – and then one of them rocketed forward. Their plan worked. The antelope panicked and ran straight to the other cheetah. A quick slash with his sharp dew claw unbalanced the prey; it hit the ground, a scurry, a pounce, and for a moment I saw nothing in the swaying golden grass. Then both cheetahs were there, one holding the antelope fast by the neck which it had tipped back, choking it. The other cheetah had already opened the antelope's stomach with its cheek teeth, but Papi assured me the poor creature was dead and not in pain. (Lions, he told me, often begin to eat while their prey is alive and still screaming!) The cheetah's dew claw, he went on, is a formidable weapon, growing just above the forepaw and bigger than a lion's – 'It's the cheetah's main killing tool, used for hooking and slashing at its prey.' We sat a while as the brothers ate, but happily not close enough to upset my – as yet – untrained and squeamish young self. Now and then they looked up towards us, disinterested, their muzzles quite red.

'What else do cheetahs have to eat here?' I asked and was told that although impalas are larger than most other antelopes, they are ideal prey, weighing up to seventy-five kilograms. Or there are gazelles at between thirty and sixty kilograms. There is a saying that where there are gazelles, there will be cheetahs! I was delighted to hear that some 50 per cent of cheetah chases end in a kill, whereas the success rate for lion hunts was only 25–30 per cent. In fact, most big cats fail more often than succeed when hunting.

There were a number of different types of antelope in Gorongosa: puku, also the size of an impala; nyala, the female – at around fifty-five to sixty kilograms and smaller than the male – ideal cheetah prey; and the tiny oribi I would come to see often on the farm. I asked about zebra foals, since I had read that cheetahs do take the young of larger animals if they can, and Ravo explained that zebras, like most large ungulates (that is, animals with hooves, herbivores), will defend their young energetically from a lone predator. But if they are attacked by three or four cheetahs and one can distract the mother, then the others will succeed in killing the foal.

'And how much of this antelope can two cheetahs eat?' I asked. Ravo replied that an adult cheetah requires four to five kilograms of meat a day but, if not interrupted, it can eat up to sixteen kilograms and will feed as long as it is left alone. This can happen in a reserve like this, Papi added, but out in the wild a cheetah can easily have its kill stolen by another predator. Young giraffes were possibly the largest prey a cheetah could take, but usually it targeted smaller animals and especially the young rather than the adults; they were easier to catch and kill, and there was less chance of their being injured.

The old park guide distracted me from the disembowelling by explaining that cheetahs are by nature solitary animals, but that sometimes a pair of litter – brothers like these will not only hunt together, but even team up with another pair or a solitary male. These young ones can bond to form a group – called 'a coalition' – and hunt together, and in this way they can bring down larger animals such as zebras or wildebeests. A male coalition can stick together for life and grows to be stronger and even lives longer than solitary cheetahs. Females usually hunt alone, though litter sisters and a mother may have overlapping home ranges; as males approach adulthood they move away from their mother's range to avoid inbreeding. The female's solitary life is one of the reasons for the decline in the cheetah populations, since a mother has to leave her small cubs in her lair while she goes and hunts for her daily ration of fresh meat. Not before they are seven to eight weeks old will she encourage them to come to watch her hunt. A litter can consist of two to six cubs, but it is rare that more than two or three survive to adulthood, except in areas where game is particularly plentiful.

Males do not stay long with the female after mating ('But sometimes they do,' said Papi with a twinkle) and the whole mating procedure is over very quickly – in about one minute. Nor does oestrus (heat) in a female cheetah last long – only about three days, shorter than with a lioness. Unlike a lioness, the female cheetah in oestrus does not advertise the fact by calling. Instead, she will leave her scent on a particular tree or anthill, then wait for the male to find her. Mating will take place in private – either in dense undergrowth or at night. Then the male will leave and not visit her again. 'He is a scoundrel, she is a lady,' said Papi. 'Not so the lioness – she will mate with more than one male in quick succession.' But he added that there was a reason for a lioness's promiscuity, since a male lion will kill cubs that are not his own. If the lioness has mated with several males, there is a chance that at least one will be the offspring of the pride's dominant lion and that might save the others. In fact, scientists now believe that cheetah females are 'promiscuous' too and that many litters contain cubs sired by more than one male. Given this, and the fact that cheetahs of both sexes roam so widely, a male meeting a female with cubs can rarely be sure that the cubs are not his, thus there is little danger of any male cheetah killing cubs.

Gestation takes about ninety to ninety-two days. The cubs are blind at birth for as long as anything between four and fourteen days, but can find their mother's teats at once, crawl at two to three days and walk at three weeks. Their mother will keep them hidden for the first six or seven weeks while she goes to hunt mornings and evenings in order to have milk to feed them. Once her cubs are seven or eight weeks old, the cheetah mother will take them with her, leaving them concealed in long grass while she hunts nearby; then she will present them with her kill to entice them to eat meat. She will bring live small game such as baby gazelles for the cubs to chase around, releasing their innate hunting skills, when they reach four to five months in age.

Cheetahs need space – those famous bursts of Olympic speed require great stretches of land, ideally desert or savannah. Like most cats, the male cheetah is territorial and, apart from his coalition partners if he has any, tries to exclude other males from his territory, but this can be hard – his home range is large, anything from 35 to 160 square kilometres. Game must be plentiful as well since, alone among the big cats, the cheetah declines to scavenge and eat meat that has not been freshly killed. A leopard carrying an antelope up into a tree and wedging it there in the fork to feast on for days, as I had seen one do on my first day on safari, is quite usual. A pride of lions will attack and kill a large animal – a hippopotamus, a buffalo, an eland or a sable antelope – and spend days feeding on the carcass. I have seen a hippo chased into a pond hoping to escape a pride of lions, not realising that they would even go into the water to kill and eat it. That hippo had lions sitting on it in the water as well as swimming around it, all chewing happily for a week. The smell was unbearable and quite near our camp!

If challenged while eating by a bigger, stronger animal, a cheetah will not stay to protect its kill for fear of being wounded in a fight. Any wound to a cheetah's legs would prevent it from hunting and it would starve. If disturbed at a kill by say, one hyena or a jackal, the cheetah will try to run it off, though not always successfully, but if faced with more than one, it will abandon its prize and be obliged to hunt again.

On the other hand, a cheetah mother is extraordinarily brave and will always protect her cubs from a predator if she can, leading it away to chase her instead. But if she does not succeed, she must resign herself to the cubs' loss; wounded, she is no good to them or to herself. Soon she will come into oestrus again to mate and three months later she can produce another litter. Nature is not sentimental and, I believe, among land mammals, only elephants, baboons and giraffes actually mourn their dead.

Sitting with Papi over the campfire during that first safari, I learned such a lot about African wildlife, including, of course, cheetahs. Born with claws like a cat, as cubs they can climb a tree to escape danger such as the arrival of a predator – a hyena, jackal or African wild dog. At about eighteen months, their claws begin to become blunt and resemble those of a dog more than a cat; shorter and straighter than those of other big cats, they remain only semi-retractable, lacking the sheath of skin that covers the claws of lions and leopards. It is one of the reasons the cheetah can run so fast: as with dogs, straighter claws give it more purchase to push off with each stride than would a paw with fully retractable claws. The longitudinal ridges on the hard, pointed pads of the feet function like cleats on a running shoe, providing traction and grip during fast turns. A cheetah's hind paws have a ridged pad as tough as a car tyre that enables it to have a firm grip at high speeds as well as aiding its explosive acceleration. With its speed coming from its muscled, elongated lower limbs, a cheetah can pass seventy-five kilometres in the first few seconds. Another aid to its speed is a large heart to pump blood and large lungs for faster breathing.

Since my early Africa days, I have often watched slow-motion films of cheetahs running down their prey. Once the beast has fallen, the cheetah will twist back its neck and clamp its short canines and blunt teeth around it and choke it. Holding the fallen animal firmly by the throat, it deftly avoids the prey's sharp, dangerous and thrashing hooves. After its burst of speed – a maximum of

ABOVE With an orphaned baby cheetah at Kapama.
BELOW A very young cheetah cub showing the 'mantle' of fluffy pale hair on its back.
This is thought to disguise the cub as a fierce honey badger when hunkered down in
grass and in danger from predators.

ABOVE Three young male siblings form a coalition that gives them greater hunting strength.

ABOVE A mother and her cubs on the alert. It's unusual to find as many as five cubs in a litter; the mother is unlikely to succeed in raising more than two cubs to adulthood.

ABOVE A subadult cheetah practises its hunting skills on a gazelle fawn.
BELOW Everything about the cheetah is designed for speed.

ABOVE The distinctive tear marks are visible even in young cubs.

110 kilometres an hour for up to five hundred metres – the cheetah must still be able to breathe through its flat nose and with a struggling antelope clamped tightly in its jaws. The prey's death throes may take up to five minutes and, by the time its victim lies still, the cheetah can be left gasping for air and exhausted.

No sooner has there been a kill in the wild than the bush telegraph operates: birds of prey circle overhead, a sure signal to other predators that fresh food is available nearby. Then, before the cheetah has dragged its kill to some quiet spot under low branches, it may be challenged by another predator, eager to see what is going for free. With little time to spare, the cheetah will first chew open the soft skin of the inner thigh, using its cheek teeth like scissors. It will then eat quickly, moving to the nutritious rump, abdominal muscles and back. If the successful cat is a lactating female with cubs, she will return to her lair and feed her young. If they are watching, and she is not challenged for the kill, she may drag it under some scrub or bush and fetch them to join her. Should she have to relinquish her kill and have not yet eaten enough, she must go out to hunt again, knowing she is leaving her cubs once more alone and vulnerable. Although she will not bring meat back to her lair, her smell and that of the cubs there will still attract predators. Therefore, she will have to move her young to a fresh lair, one at a time, and often more than once, without attracting attention before she goes to hunt. With so many hurdles to overcome, small wonder the cheetah is the most vulnerable of the big cats in Africa!

Although I had seen almost every animal the country had to offer in glorious sunshine and even by the light of the full moon, I felt that Papi's and my 'bonding safari' ended far too soon. I had learned more about the African bush in four days than in all the years I had been reading about the continent's animals and their lives. Best of all, I had come to know my father better and to see him quite differently, even to admire him for his relationship to and understanding of wildlife, whereas I had always secretly deplored his hunting of it. I still did not care for the killing of animals, but I had a better understanding of the reasons for it. What I had disapproved of strongly in my heart I now felt I could rationalise; not condoning it for pleasure, but seeing how organised hunting could be justified for the preservation of wild animals.

Papi and I arrived back at the farm full of stories, and I with full notebooks. We had seen so much game, even a number of green tree snakes, ostriches running away – 'they could break your arm easily with one wing', buffaloes with calves and, best of all (other than the cheetahs), a herd of elephants with young. I could see the relief on my stepmother's face when she saw us return quite relaxed and joking – what had she feared? But Papi decided it was time for me to be handed over to the ministrations of his darling Rosemarie. I suspect he was satisfied that he had done enough 'bonding' with his demanding daughter!

CHAPTER III

W e had been back on the farm only a few days when the chief of one of the villages on our land came with the story of a baby-snatching cheetah. Chief Aboiye would become a familiar figure to me over the next two years. He appeared a dried-up old prune of a man, although I heard he was not over forty. He had, it was whispered, fathered most of the children in the neighbourhood and it seemed on our farmland as well. Since he merrily sent off an able man from each family to work for us to pay for his taxes, he would 'look after' their wives while the husbands were in the fields. We didn't hear any complaints from the village, but then it was none of our business. It was the priest of our tiny local town who told us about Chief Aboiye's 'little habit' when he came to lunch and we all laughed when the good Father explained: 'More Christian souls for God.'

Now here stood the chief on one leg, the other foot's instep tucked on to the inside of his knee, while he leaned on his stick – his usual business stance. His problem? Rosemarie whispered to me that this was initially a social call and its true purpose would therefore take a while to come out during much farming conversation. I was to have tea with her – using the yellow tea service I came to love – and leave Papi with the chief on the terrace facing the lawn.

When Papi joined us some time later, he told us with a sigh that the village was being 'plagued' by a cheetah with a damaged foot. Since it could not run to hunt, the cheetah, he was told, had apparently taken a child from the village. This he disputed; cheetahs do not eat human flesh, but the chief had insisted that this cheetah was so hungry it had taken a baby from a hut and made off with it when no one was looking. It seemed a very unlikely story, but Chief Aboiye, a renowned negotiator and clearly a clever man, had heard that Papi had shot a lioness to save my life: surely he would be willing to shoot a big cat which had taken one of his children from a hut? Papi made us laugh by telling us he had replied that the chief was making too many babies and that the cheetah was a sign of God's disapproval. This met with the chief's ribald laughter and a slap on his knee amid much shaking of his staff. Still, Papi had agreed to go and see if he could find the baby-eating cheetah. If it really did have a damaged hind leg – caught in a trap surely set by the villagers themselves – and was no longer able to hunt, then it was probably better to put it out of its misery, baby killer or not.

I will never forget walking with Papi and his hunters, Ravo, Assia and Rodrigo, down the escarpment below the big balcony of the house towards the village in the valley. It was late afternoon and as night would fall fast we carried torches so as not to trip on tree roots or other hazards. I had no idea what to expect and was quite excited – a human-eating cheetah? Were we in danger? No, not with Papi and our three hunters all armed. Would the cheetah stalk us and then spring? No, the chief said her back leg was so badly damaged she could barely walk. Poor thing. I knew Papi intended to shoot her since she could no longer hunt to feed herself; if not, he would have no peace from the chief.

When we arrived near the village, Papi indicated to me that I should be careful how I placed my feet so as not to make a noise, and then we hunkered down not far from the entrance to the village boma. I could just make out the rondavals (round mud huts) with their thatched roofs, a little smoke curling up from the hole in the centre, showing cooking was going on inside. No one was to be seen. Were they all so afraid that even the chickens and dogs were shut in their huts? I squatted in a most uncomfortable position, something scratching my ankle through my sock. Papi and the hunters stared straight ahead, but I could see nothing in the rapidly descending darkness. Slowly Papi rose on to one knee, raised his rifle – and still I saw nothing. He fired once. Ravo indicated with an upturned thumb that the animal was dead. We all got up and walked over to the body. I was overcome by a great sadness. My first close view of a cheetah was of a dead one, still warm. When I looked at its badly lacerated, infected hind foot, however, I understood that this one was better off dead.

Papi broke the spell by turning the animal over and we saw at once from her nipples that she was lactating. Hearing the shot, the villagers had rushed out in triumph, holding flaming torches and ululating – but what a sad sight. Papi looked angry and said he would take the carcass – they were not to have the skin. A cheetah skin was a worthwhile trophy, either to sell or for their chief to wear in ceremonials. The farm was not really situated in good cheetah country – too heavily forested in the uncultivated parts – and therefore cheetahs were more prized than if they had been plentiful. Looking at the emaciated corpse, Papi knew in his heart, he told me later, that, as he had suspected, it was a trap laid by the villagers that had brought her to this miserable end (although it had probably been intended for antelope). But for her leg wound she would never have come near their village and Papi gave Chief Aboiye quite a lecture which ended in a vain threat that, if he heard of them laying any more traps on his land, they would have to leave and go elsewhere to live. (He told me afterwards that his life was not worth throwing them out, but it might just deter them.)

Then Papi sent our hunters to search for the cheetah's lair. They found it easily: no remains of a child, just some chicken feathers and a few small animal bones. 'Find her cubs before the villagers do,' Papi ordered. The men disappeared silently into the bush once more and returned within a short time carrying a tiny cub, her eyes not yet open, mewing and hissing plaintively. I reached for her and she hissed and spat at me, just as the feral kittens did in the kitchen yard.

She was so small, she could not have been more than a few days old. (I did not know then that the cub was female, but since she was I am writing 'she'.) Papi took her and handed her to me; she fitted easily into the palm of my gloved right hand, as I held her gently, my other hand forming a covering over her. But I blanched when I heard Papi say, 'There you are, this will give you something to do.' Now that I know much more about baby cheetahs than I did then, I am amazed at my confidence – and that of my father and stepmother in leaving me in charge of this small creature. I knew nothing about bringing up a baby cheetah or any tiny wild animal, but I had always loved cats, and she looked so helpless…

Into the village we walked, where Papi announced angrily that *he* would take the cub and we would take the mother's carcass with us now as well, making it clear he did not trust them to take care of either. (I still have the mother cheetah's skin, beautifully mounted by the distinguished firm of Rowland Ward and lying on the carpet in the room where I am writing – sentimental, I guess.) Papi had no doubt the cub would not survive long in the villagers' hands or that, if it did, they would surely sell it in Beira for the growing, shocking trade in wild animals.

Perhaps what surprised me most in those early days at Maforga was the lack of connection between the local people and wildlife in general. Chief Aboiye was no exception: animals were a source of food, occasionally medicine, but mostly trophies and hides to sell; This was a stark contrast to the deep love of nature and all the creatures in it that I had observed in my father on our 'bonding' safari. I had always seen him as a well-known expert on the complicated subject of hunting in both Europe and Africa, but I abhorred killing animals and so had set my mind somewhat against him and the rest of my hunting family. Despite all I had been told and had had explained to me about the practical conservation reasons for hunting – and I had heard a lot in my short life, coming as I did from a family of serious hunters on my mother's side – I still had not accepted the killing of animals in the wild except for food. Seeing and listening to my father on that first safari really changed my view of him. Instead of feeling abhorrence for the killing that he did, I began to understand his true, deep compassion for all living things and his great knowledge and interest in every aspect of their lives – and deaths. I would think on this long and hard during the next months...

Slowly we walked home, the hunters carrying the dead cheetah and I cradling the little one, one gloved hand over the other while she continued mewing, spitting, hissing, probably terrified. Rosemarie had heard the shot and was waiting on the lawn as we arrived with the carcass, but my little bundle *was* a surprise and she cooed with delight. 'Now this will be a challenge for you. Hmmm, I think we will need some help, don't you?'

I was almost speechless with the weight of my responsibility and desperate for her reassurance. 'Oh yes, all the help we can,' I remember mumbling, afraid the tiny creature would not even make it through the night.

Once inside I saw by the bright light of our pressure lamps that the cub fitted easily into the palm of my hand, snuggled there with her eyes tight shut, a little black stripe running from the inner corner of each eye down to the side of her minuscule mouth. She had a black nose, a tawny hairy back, tiny black spots on her darkish coat and, surprisingly, a dark tummy. Her paws had quite sharp transparent little hooks for claws, and a short thick, pointed tail stuck out at the end of her body. All my maternal instincts went into overdrive – I was in love and helpless with a yearning to protect her, feed her, do anything I could to ensure she survived.

Of course I had not prepared to bring home a baby cheetah and nothing was ready for her, but it did not take long for us to arrange an old cardigan of Rosemarie's into a shoe box, put this next to my bed and settle the cub in it. Papi had been watching me and exchanging looks with Rosemarie; I knew something was coming.

'Well, this will keep you busy and for some time if she lives,' said Papi, his tone less gruff than usual. 'But, darling girl, I want you to understand two things from the start, from right now. First of all, the cub will most probably die. But *if* she lives, she is *not* to be a pet. When and if she grows, she must be returned to the wild.' He held up his hand as I made to protest. 'No, not now, not yet, but when she is old enough to look after herself. This is a wild animal and must remain one. Her place is in the wild and she deserves to be returned to the wild. Do not make her a pet or you will destroy her, and she will break your heart. You cannot spend the next ten, twelve years living with a cheetah – and they can live up to twenty if well cared for. You have another life waiting for you away from here. Do you understand?' He looked so serious and almost softened.

I well remember how my heart sank, but I knew he was right. I was seventeen – twenty years of living with a cheetah on his farm? And I knew I was no Karen Blixen. But his words took some of the joy away from my intense, overwhelming happiness and I must have looked crestfallen, sitting on the floor, stroking the tiny thing with one finger, so that Rosemarie said quickly, 'Then let us get the poor little orphan something to drink. I will dilute some powdered milk while you stay with her.' And with that she dragged my father away.

Soon she was back with a bowl of warm milk and an eye dropper. 'This is the best I can do for now, but what she needs is milk and lots of it – in small doses. She would have been feeding on and off most of the night from her mother, though I doubt that poor starved creature had a lot to give. You won't get much sleep tonight, because she will let you know when she wants more.' But how? Mewing? And what a plaintive, sharp sound it was! Finally, after giving her as much milk as she could take, I ignored my bed and mosquito net, lay down on the floor next to her, a pillow under my head, and dozed.

Rosemarie was right: that first night was a sleepless one for me. The tiny creature woke often, mewing for her mother, breaking my heart. I would feed her, wipe her little bottom with torn cotton squares Rosemarie had quickly made for me, cuddle her and, when she settled, put her gently back in her soft bed. I must have been up a dozen times and although I did eventually climb on to my bed – the floor was very hard, with just rush matting and a rug on top – I did not even bother to lower my mosquito net after the first few times. She was so small and helpless, just like any newborn kitten, and very hungry that I guessed her mother had not had much milk to give her, so I fed her whenever she asked.

If I was exhausted in the morning, the cub woke quite sprightly, kneading and clawing the cardigan on which she lay and mewing gently – and no longer the wretched object of our pity. During the night, I had decided on her name. Cheetahs are known to be fast and, full of my new role as her guardian, I grandly named the little thing that could hardly crawl *Vitesse* – speed. Naturally, she became known as Tess.

Rosemarie came in early to my room with warm milk and I filled her in on my night. To my relief she offered to stay and take over from me. I fell asleep at once, leaving Tess to her.

And then I had some good luck. Our local vet, a young Portuguese called Eduardo, came as soon as he heard of my having adopted a baby cheetah – the bush telegraph works fast. He had spent several years attached to a large breeding centre near Cape Town and knew a great deal about the big cats – and he spoke English. Relief! Also, Rosemarie had a close friend named Benedita, a beautiful, elegant Portuguese lady I came to know and admire, who had successfully reared a cheetah cub and had kept the tame animal all its life on her farm near Beira. To my good fortune, Rosemarie was planning to meet her there the very day after Tess's arrival and offered to take a letter full of questions from me. Benedita replied very quickly, a long missive from which I learned the basics of mothering a baby cheetah. Between the two of them, Eduardo and Benedita – not to mention the *Encyclopaedia Britannica*, which I would scour when I had the time – I felt confident I would receive the advice I desperately needed.

On his first visit, Eduardo brought a most useful, strange, L-shaped glass bottle, very small and far more practical than the eye dropper I had been using. It was made to help vets feed newborn kittens and puppies lacking a mother and was perfect for Tess, as well as quicker. It did not take the greedy cub long to master the trick of holding one end with me and sucking from the tube. The most important thing Eduardo taught me that morning was something which would never have occurred to me. Rosemarie had given me small pieces of bandages to keep Tess clean, but I had not understood that mother cheetahs constantly lick their cubs (even their faeces). Without this encouragement to their bowels, the young can become constipated and die. I took bandages from our little clinic and cut a stack of squares from them. I placed bowls of water in a line on paper in my room, ready to wipe and massage little Tess's bottom as if I were her true mother. To my relief, that seemed to work.

I had not considered a litter tray as yet – she was still too small to crawl – but after about ten days I did, despite having been warned it was unlikely to work. To everyone's surprise, in due course Tess became thoroughly house-trained. Knowing only domestic cats and how clean they are by nature, perhaps I was less surprised than the experts when my little wild one took to the litter tray, although she showed no inclination to bury the result.

But much more urgent than house-training was what to feed her. As well as powdered milk, we had tinned condensed milk and we tried a mixture of powder and diluted condensed, which she drank greedily. For now the shoe box lined with Rosemarie's cardigan made a snug bed next to mine, the box placed just outside my mosquito net on the floor.

Those first days were very tiring; Rosemarie laughed at my exhaustion – 'just wait until you have to feed a baby of your own out here in the bush' – and I promised myself right then that would never happen. Tess slept a lot, but never long enough for me to get a few hours myself. Rosemarie came when she could to relieve me and let me sleep a little and, as long as the warm milk came, Tess did not seem to mind the different hands and smell. She was so tiny and so utterly helpless – I had no resistance. But how long would this go on? I was sleepwalking from day to day just to make sure she survived.

During that first week, Rosemarie would go out with Papi in the early mornings as usual, then come back as quickly as she could to relieve me of my night-nurse duties. When Papi drove up to the house at around nine o'clock, it was breakfast time, and Rosemarie woke me, Tess in her arms and still wrapped in the old cardigan, having enjoyed half a cup of milk.

After a few days, Rosemarie and I introduced the cub to the indoor dogs – the boxers. The ridgebacks were the 'outdoor boys', but the boxers came indoors and were far more possessive of their masters and the contents of the house. It was important for them to know from the beginning that Tess was a treasured new member of the household and not a toy. Also indoors we had a female ridgeback called Daisy, a gentle bitch, perhaps the only gentle one among them, and being the mother of the other four, all male, she was respected. It was Rosemarie's idea that we should try to see if Daisy would adopt little Tess and she felt their meeting had been a success. Daisy had sniffed, Tess had spat, but finally, when Daisy licked a reluctant Tess, Rosemarie said, 'I believe this will work,' as she handed me back the cub.

After a few more days, I dared to allow Daisy into my room in the hope that she might help me. 'Daisy will be an excellent surrogate mother, especially later when Tess needs to play. And she can protect Tess from her boys!'

'How can I stop Calypso becoming jealous?' I worried. Since I had been her 'mother' until then, and she had rarely left my side, it was a relief when Rosemarie offered to take over from me. The dogs adored Rosemarie – she was the 'pack mother' – and they all obeyed her. Happily, Calypso was evidently honoured to be taken to Rosemarie's bedroom for a week, instead of any of the other boxers – and after that she never left my stepmother to come to my quarters again. I had felt a tiny bit guilty abandoning my gift puppy, but Tess absorbed me fully from then on.

That first week, when I spent all day and every night caring for the little cub, I could not have managed without Eduardo's guidance. Oh, how I welcomed his daily visits! He advised me to mix a little egg yolk into her milk, as well as crushed vitamins he added to her bottle to compensate for the lack of nutrients from her mother. Later, he said, when she was taken outside on to the grass, she would encounter worms and bugs, and her immune system must begin building up from the beginning.

When Papi noticed Daisy had moved into my room, he asked with a certain male disdain, 'Why should a ridgeback be willing to adopt a baby cheetah? She has had her own puppies and knows this is certainly not one of them.' But, amazing as it seemed, she did – and even licked little Tess all over, just as her mother would have done. Such a relief for me! Watching Daisy carefully turning the cub with her nose and tongue to clean her and then encouraging her to crawl, pushing Tess with her nose on to all fours, surprised me completely.

Between the loving and feeding, it did not take long before Tess was as tame and dependent as a domestic kitten, following me, crawling slowly around my bedroom, dressing room and bathroom area on wobbly little legs, chirping softly, occasionally plaintively. Then I would pick her up and wash her just as I had been taught by both Eduardo and Benedita. Benedita had replied promptly to yet another of my letters and her information was invaluable, since she had also played the full-time maternity role. I noted in my journal that in those first weeks I never slept more than two hours at a stretch before Tess would wake and demand milk or attention. Her little face was smooth, but almost all of her back was covered in a sort of fluff – not as strong as fur on a coat, and a beige-honey-grey in colour. Eduardo explained that this was called a 'mantle'. Even today, no one seems quite sure why cheetah cubs grow this extra fluffy coat on their backs, but one theory is that it forms a camouflage when their mother takes them out hunting with her. She leaves them squatting in long grass until she is done and is ready to escort them back to their lair. If alone and threatened from above by birds of prey, the cubs can hunker down and their thick mantle makes them look a bit like a honey badger, a fierce little animal that not even birds of prey like to take on. In the heat of the East African summer, I wondered at nature's wisdom in adding an extra blanket to the little cheetah's coat, but perhaps this was the answer. On her tummy, legs and tail Tess had shorter, dark fur with a thick congregation of black spots. Her tail was short, bony and thick, nothing like the long, elegant rudder it would become. But while her walk was still quite unsteady, and she would often topple over and sit, that little tail, as thick as my forefinger, already stuck out and was used to balance her.

Once I had begun letting Daisy into my room, she, too, had become a member of the family and I called her 'Aunty Daisy' when talking about her to Tess – which I did all the time, telling her stories and generally 'rabbiting on', as Papi said with a growl as we sat down at table, but I knew he was pleased I was happily engaged.

After that first week, I was exhausted. I had just enough energy to crawl under my mosquito net and into my bed, with Tess curled up in the box on an ever-changing bed of old pullovers, constantly being washed. Papi came into my room a few times to make sure she was not actually sleeping in my bed or on it, that I was keeping her outside the mosquito net and next to it. I realised he was completely serious about my not making a pet of her – but it was hard.

Whenever Tess slept during the day, I read and took notes about cheetahs. Since I was her primary source of milk and – apart from Daisy – affection, instead of purring like a cat as I had expected, she constantly made a peculiar chirping sound, a high-pitched baby-birdlike noise, or uttered tiny yelps or yips, which easily charmed everyone. Eduardo, soon my good friend, told me that when she was able to see me, Tess would recognise me and trust me as her mother. Thereafter, he assured me, she would obey – a tap on the nose and a sharp 'no' would be imprinted at once on her consciousness. 'Cats, like most animals, have memory rather than intelligence,' he explained, and I have found this true in most cases. But the thought of Tess recognising me and obeying…? I lived in a daze of optimistic hope.

Each day I would wake to a new development in my young charge. When her eyes opened, everything changed. Her mewing became more demanding, she recognised my finger first and then slowly my face and smell. Eduardo told me cheetahs do not have a good sense of smell, the bone structure of their skull being too flat, but since scent-marking is important to all cats, theirs was attuned to their particular sensory needs. Tess's purring, on the in and out breath unlike a domestic cat's, increased with her yowling. Desperate that she missed her mother's love and the companionship of siblings, Daisy and I did our best to compensate with attention. I even imitated purring! Eduardo assured me that in the wild her mother would have had to leave the cub twice a day to hunt for her own food, so that I should not be afraid to leave Tess alone. But even during meals, I could hear her mewing from my room, which was next to the dining area of the large L-shaped living room. As I made to get up and go to her, 'Stay,' Papi would order with a glare and, like a good dog, I would sit down again, fidgeting. He was right, of course, though I thought him cruel and would make appealing eye contact with Rosemarie. But she never argued with him and did not return my plaintive looks.

Eduardo reckoned that when Tess's eyes opened she must have been about ten or eleven days old, although her ears with their black spot on the back were still flat against her head and level with her eyes. The typical black tear streaks which mark all cheetahs, running from the inner eye down to the mouth, had been visible since the first moment I saw her. No one seems to know why cheetahs have this feature; Eduardo believed the theory that it saved them from the sun's glare since they hunt by day, unlike all the other big cats.

Another theory is that the tear marks help their 'aim' when hunting, as sights do on a rifle. Papi thought this theory had some merit.

After that first anxious week, neither my stepmother nor my father came more often than every few days to see what I was up to, although I knew Rosemarie was ready to drop anything to join me if I asked. She was terribly excited about having little Tess in our lives and later I realised how much she wanted to share her with me. Initially I was too busy to notice, but after a while I understood how content they both were that I was occupied. Keeping me interested in something on the farm had been their greatest worry about having me to stay with them. They would go out very early, before the day's heat began, to their separate areas of the farm, to discuss the work programme with the foremen and to give them their instructions: the farm was large and the two of them divided responsibility for the many different crops and fruit between them. I first saw them around nine in the morning, when they returned for breakfast, always full of stories, some joyful, others less so.

Rosemarie came in one morning with stunning news. 'The police in the north have caught the man who tried to kill Papi a year ago.'

It had happened like this. One day, when getting into Papi's Land Rover, Rosemarie saw blood stains in the centre of the driver's seat's canvas cover. No one except Papi drove that car and he had used it earlier that day. Then she noticd that his khaki shorts also had blood stains on the back. When she asked him about this, he had no idea how or why and said he felt fine, but agreed to go with her to the clinic. Following an examination, the doctor insisted he remain in bed there. Over the next week, the bleeding became heavier and, after two weeks with no improvement and following all the examinations, it became clear my father was losing blood at such a rate that he would surely die. Rosemarie had sent for a doctor from Johannesburg and another from Salisbury, but neither could explain the cause or offer a solution. When Papi fell into a coma, and Rosemarie was distraught, Antonio the cook came to her and, after much shifting of feet and embarrassment, offered his brother, a witch doctor, to help heal 'Ba'as'. In her desperation, Rosemarie agreed to see him – a 'white witch doctor', she told me: in other words, one who 'invoked the spirits for good, not evil'. Since Papi was much too pragmatic to believe in 'such nonsense' and Rosemarie too Catholic, it was a difficult decision for her.

But Antonio was an honest-looking man, a good churchgoer, and had been on the farm with Papi from the beginning. She felt she had nothing to lose (other than a month's salary for the house staff). She was very doubtful about the 'dark arts', and with Papi a total disbeliever they had never become involved in the 'spirit world' of their employees. I was fascinated with the concept of witch doctors in general, and listened in awe. Antonio's brother, Roberto, had arrived that evening. He knew the story of Papi's inexplicable bleeding, said he could cure him – and named a rather large sum for the process. Rosemarie knew that this was the way these magic men worked – first you pay and then (maybe) they succeed. So she paid and drove with Roberto to the clinic. Once there, he asked to be left alone with Papi, but Rosemarie insisted the door was left open. She heard chanting and shuffling as if Roberto was dancing, looked in and, during his performance, saw him sprinkling something like water over my unresponsive father.

After about ten more minutes, Roberto came out smiling and announced that Papi was 'cured'. A sceptical Rosemarie saw him still comatose, left and drove back to the farm in silence. As she deposited Roberto with Antonio in the kitchen yard, she heard shouts of glee and merriment, but retired sadly to her room, the house dogs with her.

The next day when she arrived at the clinic, to her amazement Papi was sitting up in bed eating breakfast! The doctors were astounded, he was definitely better and the haemorrhaging had stopped. The following day, my father said he wanted to go back home with her, that he felt quite well. To her surprise, the doctors agreed – they could find nothing wrong with him, but still had no explanation for his almost bleeding to death and then mysteriously recovering.

Some two weeks later, Antonio came out from his kitchen lair again – he almost never entered the house proper, let alone the dining area – and passed on to Papi and Rosemarie what his brother had told him. My father, he alleged, had had 'a bad spell' put on him by someone who wanted revenge, someone who had been dismissed from the farm. Did they know who that might be? After further probing Antonio said that it seemed this man was now in the north of the country. Surely they remembered? He could be recognised by a distinctive scar on his ear and neck. Neither Antonio nor his brother had ever seen this man nor had any idea of his name, but perhaps he could be identified.

Less sceptical now, and with that information, Papi told the police. He remembered the man, but doubted he carried a grudge: the worker had himself admitted his crime of theft and accepted his dismissal. It was said he had left the farm laughing. Rosemarie thought more of it than Papi, found out the man's name and gave it to the police, as well as his possible location. Due to the identifying scar, it did not take them long to find him. In exchange for a lighter sentence for a new misdemeanour, he promised to give them the name of the 'black witch doctor' who had made up the lethal powder to be sprinkled somewhere only Papi would sit – the seat of his Land Rover had been ideal. This powder would cause certain death – and he also gave the police the name of someone else who, he said, had paid for the powder. Following this lead, the police did not take long to discover that it was Papi's former employee, the man with the scar, who was the criminal, not the person he had blamed. The culprit confessed and was subsequently sentenced.

This story brought home to me for the first time the power of witch doctors, for good and evil; so much so that, some six months later, when I was semi-delirious in the Rhodesian bush and was offered treatment by one, I did not resist. And I would be party to other quite remarkable instances as well.

Not every breakfast time brought such dramatic stories, but each day I would regale Papi and Rosemarie with Tess's progress, just like the nanny of a first-time baby reporting to its parents. They didn't always pay much attention – there was a lot of farm business to discuss – but I soon realised it wasn't that they were indifferent; on the contrary, they were both delighted and relieved, they told me later, to see how happy I was with my new responsibility. Since the dogs were usually with them and, apart from Daisy, did not come into my area anyway, I felt my little Tess was quite secure with me.

After a couple of weeks, even the tiny L-shaped bottles were taking too long to feed Tess, and I bought three baby's bottles from the village store with a number of teats – I had been warned these would not last long once the cub's teeth began to grow at around four weeks old, but they were fine for the time being. The bottle and teat worked better than the L-shaped glass if I held the bottle, but Tess kept kneading against my hands, and by now she had sharp little claws. I remembered how kittens knead their mother's stomach when drinking, pushing in and out with their paws, but although I wore my fingerless cotton gloves, my hands were quite scratched and raw. I had to devise an alternative and buttonholed our carpenter. Joao was always inventive and, with his help, I attached some thick foam from a packing crate on to a small rectangular wooden board he cut for me and made a hole in the centre for the bottle's rubber teat to come through. While I held the bottle from behind the board, Tess could now push on the foam on either side of the teat as if it were her mother's stomach. Even though the foam or a substitute had to be replaced often, it was a relief, as I dared not use any ointment on my scratches in case Tess licked it off. At this stage she still had no teeth – and I put my little finger in her mouth when she crawled on to me while I sat on the floor reading, leaning against the bed with my head propped against a pillow on the side of the metal frame. There she would suckle my finger hopefully before falling asleep, which she did much of the time. Once when Rosemarie came in she burst out laughing, left and came back with her camera to record the sight of me sitting on the floor with a book in one hand, my back against the bed and the baby cheetah sleeping on my lap with the little finger of my other hand still in her mouth. How I would love that photo now.

My first African Christmas was unforgettable. It was incredibly hot and humid, which I did not like at all. Attending church was a test of devotion – no windows opened and the heat and smell of perspiration from the packed benches made concentrating on the service difficult. But the singing was angelic and the energetic dancing down the aisles by the congregation in their colourful best was visually glorious and presented a most unusual sight to a convent-reared girl. The local Catholic mission had a good following and the children, all dressed in white with their brilliant smiles, were a joy.

Rosemarie and I took hours decorating the Christmas tree with lametta, a sort of thin silver fettuccine which we hung, one strand at a time, to create a glittering skirt on each branch, waving gently in the slight breeze from the open balcony windows. We sighed with pleasure when it was finished and then I added the candles – wax ones, naturally. On Christmas Eve, I had rather a surprise. In the heat, the candles had softened, bent over and were now facing the floor! 'Oh dear – yes, we usually put them up at the last minute to light, sing some carols and then blow them out,' a laughing Rosemarie told me.

It was not only the candles that were affected by the Christmas humidity. My leather shoes, bags and belts all acquired mildew, as did anything leather inside the house. Still, we would sit on the veranda after dinner and the breeze coming up the valley from the coast was pleasantly cool after the heat of the day. Tess was far too small to partake of the Christmas season, but I left the door to my suite of rooms open for her to join us if she wanted and sometimes she did.

On New Year's Eve I joined in another tradition Tess could not appreciate that first year. We decorated the back frames of our chairs by winding a twist of pretty leaves round them. Then, just before midnight, we stood on the seats of our chairs, waiting. When we heard the stroke of midnight from the wireless (attached to the battery removed from the Land Rover), we jumped down and *into* the New Year. I am not sure if this was one of Rosemarie's inventions, but I loved it. Benedita had come to spend the holiday with us, which was a joy for Rosemarie and Papi and a godsend for me – I had been begging her by telegraph. Now I would really learn how best to care for our little one.

Tess was about four to five weeks old and it was at this time that I first heard a new sound from her, a sort of chirping; Benedita told me that cheetahs often appear to imitate bird calls. To attract them so they can catch them? Neither she nor Eduardo seemed to know, but I began to realise that when I was in one of the other rooms of her/my territory, Tess was calling me. Another strange thing was that, whenever I left her alone in my room, I would return to find her sitting upright, legs side by side in front of her, exactly where I had left her. This, I discovered, is what cubs do in the wild: they stay exactly where their mother has left them for their safety in case of predators, and wait patiently for her return.

Once Tess grew out of her shoe box, she seemed content to sleep on a rug I placed beside my bed, with the blanket from her box on top so that the smell was familiar. No matter how much I longed to have her on my bed, Benedita had stressed the need to keep Tess as independent as possible. I knew in my heart that Papi had spoken wisely when he told me she would have to be released into the wild one day, obliged to fend for herself. No, I could not allow her to become a dependent pet. I too would leave, but I pushed that thought as far away as possible. Anything could happen, I thought with the optimism typical of the young.

Tess was incredibly affectionate – much more so, Benedita told me, than her own cub had been, but Tess had come to me much younger. She loved to feel my nails scratch lightly along her spine, just like any domestic cat. I was fascinated by the large black spot she had on the back of each ear and longed to stroke it, but she did not like me to touch her ears and I didn't do it again. Her chirrup was the most delicious sound, a sweet high-pitched trilling. In time, as she grew, her purr became a deep roll of mini-thunder. The purr of a cat is particularly pleasing, but surprisingly the purr of a cheetah – a beautifully rhythmic, loud, rolling noise – does not necessarily mean happiness. I have been told by those who know that it has even been heard in alarm or in anger.

Those early days, then weeks, before Tess was jumping about and climbing anything and everything, were among the happiest of my life. This adorable little creature was totally reliant on me and I doted on her every need. She still slept a lot and I took that free time to study the life and history of the cheetah.

Here is what I gleaned at this time from Rosemarie's *Encyclopaedia Britannica* and jotted down:

> *Cheetah: Belonging to the subfamily Felinae and the family Felidae, its Latin name is* **Acinonyx jubatus** *and it is the only member of the* **Acinonyx** *genus.*

Thanks to my Classicist son, I now know that the cheetah's generic name of *Acinonyx* may have come from the combination of three Greek words roughly translated to mean 'non-moving claws'. *Jubatus* in Latin means 'maned', which would refer to the cheetah's dorsal crest, the remainder of their baby mantle and still visible like a short mane at fifteen months, even later sometimes. Other members of Felinae belong to the genus *Felis*, which includes small and medium-sized cats such as the cougar, lynx and domesticated varieties, while the big cats – tigers, lions, leopards, jaguars and the slightly smaller snow leopards and clouded leopards – belong to another subfamily, Pantherinae, and to the genus *Panthera*. This group diverged from the rest of the cat family about two to three million years ago.

There are divergent views about the evolution of the cheetah. A recent genome study concluded that it originated in North America and spread to Asia and Africa around 100,000 years ago. As a result of this first migration a genetic bottleneck formed in the population and cheetahs became extinct in North America at the end of the last Ice Age. Supporters of this theory today claim that it is illustrated by the allegation that, due to their close relationship, cheetahs can accept a skin graft from any other cheetah without it being rejected.

The other popular view is that the cheetah emerged in Africa as early as the Miocene epoch (26 million to 7.5 million years ago), as did the sabre-toothed cat. During the Lower Pleistocene (2.5 million to 780,000 years ago), a giant cheetah (*Acinonyx pardinensis*) roamed in Europe, India and China; then in the Middle Pleistocene (780,000 to 126,000 years ago) a smaller form (*Acinonyx intermedius*) evolved. This ranged as far east as China, while during the same period the sabre-toothed cats declined.

Around 200,000 years ago, the cheetah as we know it today, smaller than *A. intermedius* and classified as *Acinonyx jubatus,* ranged through China and India. Then at the close of the last Ice Age, around 11,700 years ago, this too became extinct in eastern Asia. Meanwhile it and the other cat predators became widespread in Africa, India and southwestern Asia – enabling us to conclude that there must have been sufficient wild game for them all. As for proof, the earliest known fossil record of the cheetah was found among a number of animal fossils dating from the Lower Pleistocene in the Olduvai Gorge in Tanzania.

Despite their close relationship, there are physical differences between cheetahs: some that lived in colder climates had longer hair, while those of the Saharan areas became paler in colour, to enable them to disguise themselves better. Those that are found in woodland areas (especially when driven from more open ground and obliged to adapt) are slightly darker for the same reason.

It is true that a cheetah has a number of dog-like attributes. In addition to its claws and hard, dog-like pads, it sits upright like a dog, both forelegs planted straight in front of its body, and hunts like a dog as well. But it really does belong in a class of its own. A racehorse can run at about sixty kilometres an hour for three kilometres or so; a cheetah can reach 110 kilometres an hour, making it the world's fastest mammal – but only for a short distance, about five hundred metres maximum, with each stride covering seven metres at full speed, about the same as a galloping horse. Some gazelles can run at ninety kilometres an hour and can maintain that speed for much longer than a cheetah. For this reason the cheetah first stalks its prey, leaving itself a shorter distance to dash. If it has cover it will try to creep up to within sixty or seventy metres of its quarry. Should the prey look up, the cheetah will drop to the ground and freeze before slowly and carefully starting to inch forward again. For a cheetah to succeed, stalking is as important as the full-speed charge. In fact, a cheetah's prey *must* flee for it to hunt successfully. A lion or a leopard can jump on to its quarry and cling to pull it down, but the cheetah, being much lighter, cannot hope to wrestle and hold on to an antelope. It needs to chase, run alongside, then use the momentum to trip its victim with its paw to make it stumble or fall. Knocking its prey over is a tricky procedure which requires expertise and precision timing – as does holding it by the neck in its jaws to choke it. Without running and tripping, the cheetah has little chance of capturing its victim.

Interestingly, the cheetah leaves behind the tidy skeleton of its prey – almost intact – since it eats the meat without chewing the bones.

At eighteen months or so, a subadult cheetah can still climb up a tree, though not well, and there is the danger of being followed by a stronger climbing predator such as a leopard. Because of its short, blunt claws, a cheetah also has difficulty getting down again and it often slides much of the way, relying on forked branches to lean against and slow its descent.

As for a cheetah's coat: the adult's has short hair, often rather coarse between its small, solid black spots, which have thicker, slightly longer hair. An adult has almost two thousand spots, each about one and a half to two centimetres across, which appear on its skin, with the hair growing black through them. (A leopard, by contrast, does not have solid spots, but rosettes with a little yellow or tan patch of fur in the centre.) A cheetah's underbelly changes from dark grey-almost-black as a cub to white at about six months. Ferreting about in the encyclopaedia I was surprised to learn that every cheetah has a unique pattern of spots on its coat, giving each animal a distinct identity.

The predominant feature of a cheetah, and that which defines it, is that it is built for speed. Its ears can flatten on its proportionally small cranium, and it has smaller teeth than other cats; the nose is flat; the bones lightweight and the limbs long. When in full flight, all four of the feet, like those of a galloping horse, leave the ground, and the hind legs and feet will stretch out in front of its body. The vertebral column is extremely supple and enables the cheetah to flex its spine and spring forward with those extraordinary bounds. As the spine curves with the action, the long tail acts like a rudder – as on a boat – to balance its body while it runs.

When I read that a mother cheetah keeps her cubs in seclusion for the first four weeks or so, I did the same, keeping Tess in my bedroom with daily visits from Daisy of course, as well as from Rosemarie when she had time, and Eduardo sometimes twice a week. Occasionally when he had been useful, I would let in my young guardian, Francisco, but *without his panga!*

Somehow the hub of the house became my bedroom. At four weeks, Tess had sharp little teeth and the rubber teats on her bottles did not last long. She started sniffing at my fingers and licking them with a soft little tongue, although I was warned that the tongue would grow sharp spikes soon enough and I would find being licked much less pleasant!

Tess was growing fast: each week I saw a considerable difference. Eduardo suggested it was time for her to have some solid food, a little meat, and Sixpence the main house cook (I never did discover how he got that name) was not pleased at having to mince the antelope meat our hunters brought in. This had to be ground by hand in the mincer and it was slow work. Mixed with milk, Tess loved it and could not get enough.

By now she had the run of my rooms – my bedroom, dressing room and bathroom, where I made sure always to close the lid on the WC, terrified she might jump up on to the seat and fall in. The bath was another great attraction when I sat in it; she loved to walk around the edge, which was one tile wide on either side and at the front where the taps stood, with a deeper ledge at the rounded end where I reclined my head. One day as I was getting out of the bath I did not hear the tiny splash. Tess had slipped in, but was out again before I could help – as if jet propelled on hitting the water! Somehow she had leaped for the chain and the soap rack across the bath and was out as quickly as she was in. I wrapped the sodden little thing in my towel and had to laugh. She looked terrible – spikey and skinny. I rubbed her dry, telling her all the while what a silly girl she was and making soothing noises as best I could. She never walked around the edge of my bath again, although later she would sit on the ledge behind my head and make her special chirruping sound.

Another week went by and Tess, who for a while now had been up and about without the need of Daisy's nose to prod her, longed to go outside. So, just like a cheetah mother taking her young out to watch her hunting, I began to carry Tess out of the house with me. At six weeks she was completely agile and steady on her feet, her legs had grown longer and she jumped about so much I decided to let her play on the big lawn in front of the house, where the driveway encircled it. The grass was cut short, which discouraged the snakes I so dreaded and also enabled us to see them – while Francisco joined us with his panga, itching to use it!

On the lawn, Tess could see something of the world and Daisy encouraged her to chase her and to play – rough and tumble. Since I had heard that was the only way cubs in the wild learn to hunt, I gently encouraged it, rolling a tennis ball for her and Daisy to compete for it. I also needed Daisy nearby to guard us both from her boisterous sons, if I could not keep them shut away. The boxers were no longer interested in Tess's wanderings about the house, but soon I realised I would have to introduce her to The Ridgeback Gang.

The ridgebacks were no more amused than the boxers had been when I held Tess for them to sniff and she spat at them energetically.

However, they understood at once that she was someone special who needed to be protected, and obeyed when I told them not to lick her or prod her with a forefoot. Eventually they played with her, always trying to avoid her sharp little claws. After our first week outdoors on the lawn with the dogs, I began to work at getting her used to wearing a body harness – a collar would be too difficult and she might choke on a lead if she climbed and became entangled. This I designed with input from Eduardo and Rosemarie, and had the local shoemaker follow my precise instructions. It was made out of soft brown leather, lined in glove leather in case it chafed her, and had many holes available for extension.

I started by putting the harness partially on while I was grooming her – I brushed her coat each day anyway, to see if she had picked up any ticks, or scratches from thorns, or if she had torn one of her nails. She loved her grooming sessions and would sit patiently as I brushed her, telling her stories as if she were a little girl. The harness had a wider leather strap across her chest which joined another around her upper stomach, coming up behind her front legs and over her upper back. There was a clip on either side of the back strap for a leather loop to be attached and in this way we could lead her. I only attached a long lead for walks, but it had several places on it where I could shorten it.

These were dangerous times as little Tess exerted her boundless energy, trying to race about with the dogs. Fortunately they were obedient and always came when called, which brought Tess back as well, invariably following Daisy. When she was tired she would sit down and refuse to walk, no matter how far we were from the house, so then I had to carry her anywhere she would not or could not go – through the long grass or on the slippery edges of our dams. I worried about the snakes as well, but Francisco became the useful guardian he was meant to be, waving his trusty panga to either side ready to protect us both. I had been assured that snakes usually get out of the way when they hear a footfall, but still...

Once she could go out at will, Tess preferred to do her business outside and, to my surprise, unlike most cats, often in exactly the same place. She preferred to squat on smooth stones in the garden, but did not cover her scat with soil as a domestic cat would do. She no longer used the litter tray, but I kept it for some time for the nights. Later I would see her part-bury the remains of a carcass in soil, although she never went back to dig it up again: perhaps to avoid attracting predators? One of her games in the garden was to try to catch butterflies in the flowerbeds, in which, to Rosemarie's dismay, she crashed about.

The water spilling gently over the edge of the dam Papi had designed and built fascinated Tess and she would try to catch it – another thing that surprised me, since I knew cheetahs do not like getting their paws wet and especially after her experience falling into my bath.

The farm was well known for its abundance of water – not only for the beautifully curved dam, but for the many little waterfalls – there was even a charming stepped cascade running down near the terrace of the house which faced the numerous valleys and hills on that 170-kilometre drive towards Beira and the coast. My father had a strange gift – he was a 'water diviner'. Nor did he need rods to help him; he just used his hands, walking with his arms extended in front of him, his fingers outstretched. When he felt a 'twinge', there he would have a hole dug and lo! water. In this way there was water wherever he wanted it on the farm and buildings, and decorative pools in the huge lawn area. Papi was inordinately proud of this gift but, since the farm was in subtropical country with plenty of rainfall, perhaps his finds were not as extraordinary as they would have been in a desert! If any guest wanted to swim they could do that in the large pool under the cascade falling from the top of the dam.

Traditionally, it seems, the gift of water divining passes from father to daughter; she then passes it to her son and so on. I was the exception. I had to stand on top of the dam before the rods would even twitch slightly. This was such a cause of shame that Papi declared I could not be his daughter and must have been switched at birth. The only way I could reassure him was to remind him that I had been born in the free hospital in Karlsbad, Bohemia, donated by my mother's uncle: I was the first baby ever born there, since my great-uncle was an orthopaedic surgeon who set bones!

In his early days on the farm, word of Papi's water-divining skills spread and soon he would receive invitations to visit various farms around the territory. Because he was a famous hunter, the owners would write lamenting that they had a particularly bold elephant or buffalo troubling their farmstead or similar: it needed shooting and could he help? Papi often obliged (happily times have changed) and then, since he was there, could he possibly deploy his great skill to test if there was any water underground in the area? Very often he was successful. Since I never showed the slightest talent in this direction I would surely not survive in the drier savannah country cheetahs love.

ABOVE Bottle-feeding a tiny orphaned cub at Kapama – as I fed baby Tess long ago.
INSET A subadult orphaned cheetah climbing on furniture – again, just like Tess.

ABOVE 'Nothing screams cute like a cheetah cub'. Hoedspruit Endangered Species Centre experienced a 'baby boom' in 2017 when five of their female cheetahs gave birth – between them a total of 17 cubs were born.
BELOW One 'king' cheetah born within a litter of four orphaned cubs.

ABOVE A mother cheetah teaches her subadult cubs how to kill a warthog.
BELOW A king's magnificent markings.

ABOVE A young king cheetah poses for the camera.
BELOW With Birman, a favourite from among the orphaned cheetahs at Kapama.

CHAPTER IV

When Tess was six weeks old, Eduardo gave her the shots he said she needed to supplement her lack of mother's milk. Then, on his urging, and after long discussions with Papi and Rosemarie and further correspondence with Benedita, I asked our two house hunters, Rodrigo and Assia, to take Tess with them now and then when they went hunting for us. She could wear her tiny harness and lead. But I quaked at leaving her alone and begged to be allowed to go as well – I would hold the lead. It would help to get her used to them, I said, and of course they had to agree.

At first the plan was that she would be allowed to watch, then be offered some of the shot animal's blood. In the wild, cheetah cubs can begin to eat meat from their mother's kill at about six weeks of age, although they may continue to suckle until about three months. They will sit where they are told, not moving but watching their mother hunt, waiting for her to call them to the kill. I had to find a way of replicating this procedure. So at going on two months old, Tess was permitted to watch when our hunters opened the shot animal's stomach; then she would be given a little to eat. The rest was for our table. At about three months, perhaps they could undo her lead from the harness and see what happened: would she crouch and begin to stalk? I was told I should not interfere with this slow progress, nor get in the way and distract her.

Since Tess had come into my care, I had had few breaks from her, nor had I wanted any. But now Papi and Rosemarie insisted I needed to get away... I could safely leave Tess with them, and with Rodrigo and Assia, who were by now devoted to her. And Aunty Daisy would sleep with her in my room.

Knowing my love of horses and competition riding, it was decided I should visit friends in Namibia (Southwest Africa in those days) who bred and trained competition horses as a sideline to breeding cattle for sale. Later I would understand I was being sent away to separate me from Tess; Papi and Rosemarie realised that my life revolved around her too intensely and that it could not continue like this for much longer. My days and nights had been reduced to nurturing this one animal – hardly the multi-faceted experience I should have been having in Africa. Protesting until Papi pushed me on to the plane, I flew to Windhoek, the capital of Namibia.

Namibia had been a German colony until World War I and on arrival to my amazement I found that many of the local people from a tribe called the Hereros, tall elegant Africans, still spoke German. The first shop I entered greeted me with a cheerful 'Gruss Gott' – 'Greet the Lord', the familiar German greeting – just as if I had been in Vienna or Munich. The Hereros came across as very friendly, especially the couple who had been sent to meet me from the small plane in which I arrived. I noticed the women in the street were unusually tall and slender compared with the smaller, stockier women of the Shona tribe on the farm, and carried themselves proudly as if supporting a water jug on their heads (which I discovered they had often done in the past). They wore exotic turbans in bright colours (on which the jug would have had to balance) and long gypsy-style skirts to the floor, while they moved slowly and gracefully, almost like dancers. I was impressed – also by their broad smiles and gleaming, even, white teeth. I learned that their fine teeth were one of their sources of pride and I was given some cut roots they used as toothbrushes to try. If it worked for them… ?

I was led to a buggy drawn by two splendid greys – part Arabian? Lipizzaners? Surely not? – waiting for me and my luggage. After a little shopping, soon we were driving out into the countryside, a flat area in the highlands and dry in March when I arrived. I had been told this was an excellent time to see game, with hot days and cool to cold nights, little if any dust and occasional rain. Although the area was flat, with hard and sandy ground, Windhoek was 1,700 metres above sea level. Excellent – I was glad to be away from the humidity of subtropical Mozambique for a while.

The Herero couple who had come to fetch me were very senior among the staff of the cattle ranch to which we were driving, so I had no hesitation in quizzing them. The cattle there were raised for beef, they told me, and were huge, with very long horns sticking out almost horizontally from their heads. Originally bred by the Africana people, they were a cross between the long-horn and the Brahman cattle, a shining deep russet colour, and they all sported a hump on the back of their neck which wobbled from side to side as they walked. My guides explained that in this strange hump the animals were able to store water in the hot dry country of the local cattle ranches. When I saw them, I remember thinking I would not like to get in the way of one of those great beasts.

As well as rearing cattle, my hosts at the ranch bred competition horses for three-day eventing, something I yearned to do. To exercise these young horses before they were sold, they invited talented young riders from all over Africa and even some from Europe to train the horses and be trained themselves under the supervision of a famous teacher. She turned out to be an ancient German countess who walked with a stick and great difficulty. After I met her and was duly in awe of her gruff manner, I asked my hosts how could she possibly sit on a horse and train them when she could hardly walk. 'You will see,' I was told. 'And don't get too near the Lipizzaner stallion she rides. He bites!' – something I confirmed to my cost a few days later.

Once the countess was mounted, everything changed. No stiffness, no concession to any crippling condition – she was a marvel on horseback and barked orders at the ten of us young pupils, rightly expecting to be obeyed. She was much more interested in our mounts and their development than in ours and made that clear at once. And it was hard work riding every day for three hours in the outdoor riding school in that heat.

The horses presented to us, their 'trainers', were superb – none more than four years old, skittish, feisty, warm-blooded – ready for working, and yes, some were part Arabian, or part Lipizzaner and part thoroughbred. All had been broken in and ridden, but none had as yet learned any of the finer disciplines of dressage or show jumping. Many were descended from the countess's stallion. 'His name is Marengo, in honour of the horse Napoleon rode at that Battle of Waterloo,' she told us, 'which was won by a German, of course!' I would learn about General Blücher – 'who came to Wellington's aid at the last minute or he might have lost to Napoleon!' The Countess's Marengo was a sort of flea-bitten grey, not large either (like the real Marengo), about fifteen and a half hands, but he had been coupled with larger thoroughbred mares to produce fast, taller jumpers. The results were not always what the breeders had in mind; some were ideal, but others had the tricky temperament of their sire and not always the jumping talent hoped for. I knew all about Lipizzaners and had been promised I could ride the young colts one day in Lipizza in Yugoslavia, their original home when it was a part of the Austrian Empire. Bred at first to execute clever movements which would enable their riders to strike yet avoid being struck in battle, they were now used to demonstrate how this was done and with the same strict military discipline still practised in the famous Spanish Riding School in Vienna. Their conformation does not lend itself to show jumping or racing and they are too intelligent for dressage competitions, learning the test before their riders, often anticipating a command before it is given; result: negative points from judges. But to my mind nothing in dressage can compete with the glorious display Lipizzaners still present in Vienna.

The group of young riders on the ranch in Namibia was fun to be with and although we had to work hard – grooming the horses both before and after riding, feeding them, seeing to their tack – in the evenings there were picnics or games and sometimes dances. But it was Sundays that I looked forward to the most; on Sundays we would ride out into the countryside with our host and watch out for wildlife, abundant in those days.

I had been there for ten days when, on my second Sunday, I saw a cheetah hunt. We had not long passed my first quiver tree, a type of aloe, when I caught sight of something moving fast and not too far away. A springbok was the target of not one but two cheetahs coming at speed on either side, copying the antelope's twisting and turning, leaping over the bushy shrubs dotting the ground, weaving this way and that. I watched as the cheetahs' tails swung from side to side to balance their own turning behind the springbok and could not believe the speed at which they ran. It did not last long – perhaps a couple of minutes, not more. Suddenly one of the pair lashed out with a paw at the springbok's hind quarters and a thin red gash appeared. This unbalanced the animal while the other cheetah reached out with its forepaw, tripping the antelope, which landed in a cloud of dust. Our leader held us all back so as not to drive off the big cats, the first gripping the struggling animal by the neck tight in its jaw while avoiding its thrashing hooves or lunges from its sharply pointed horns.

We stayed as quiet as we could, given that our somewhat agitated young mounts were unaccustomed to the predator cats. The two cheetahs paid us no mind. They were clearly used to the sight of horses – herbivores, after all, and not a threat to them – and we were on a regular exercise route from the farm. Once their prey lay still, both cheetahs set to, one starting on its rump and the other on the soft skin of its inner thigh and abdomen. All the while, our leader was telling us quietly – most of us new to seeing cheetahs at all, let alone on a hunt – that they must feed quickly before birds of prey alerted other predators to a kill by circling above it. Hyenas, wild dogs, leopards, even lions would be happy to have a cheetah do their hunting for them.

I was overwhelmingly impressed and as we rode on, circling wide around the feeding cheetahs, I picked up what facts I could. Cheetahs in Namibia were then far more numerous than I had thought, although farmers hunted them to preserve their cattle herds. There was plenty of game for the cats, but a calf was easier to catch than an antelope and when that happened farmers would shoot the cheetahs. At this time, 1962, the interest in conservation had not yet taken hold and to the cattle rancher the cheetah was a pest, as the fox is to an English farmer's lambs or chickens.

During that outing, we came upon two lions trotting determinedly along together and happily away from us, as well as a pair of eland antelope, large, amazing beasts, with thick, straight, twisted horns pointing backwards. I was told they usually travel in herds, but here were two large males, standing facing each other's rump, busily grooming one another! At the shoulder they stood taller than our horses and, being heavier and larger, they are slower than other antelopes. They have about fifteen vertical white stripes travelling down from their spines to their stomachs on either side of their roan-brown coats, and long black and brown manes growing from the top of their heads to the middle of their backs. Astonishingly, they can jump up to two and a half metres from standstill if startled.

I never imagined they would be so magnificent. Eland are prey to lions and African wild dogs, both of which hunt in groups; a pair or coalition of cheetahs may attack one, but they are too big for a lone cheetah to tackle. What one learned on those Sunday rides out! I also saw my first sable antelopes, males with coats a dark reddish brown, their elegant curved horns reaching back towards their rump, even more beautiful than the kudu I had seen in Mozambique. But as I rode back to the farm my thoughts were full of that dazzling cheetah chase I had witnessed.

In those days, some sixty years ago, cheetahs were easy to spot on the open savannah. During a number of visits there in the course of my life, I have often seen them, even with subadult young they were teaching to hunt. And once, on that first visit, I watched a mother bring a wounded steenbok antelope to her four almost grown cubs and saw how she allowed them to play with it like a cat with a mouse until one of them choked it, holding the neck in its jaws. This was an important lesson for me to take home: mother cheetahs teach their young how to hunt and then kill… Until that time I had known that cubs, once weaned at about three or four months, would watch their mother, but not that she actually brought wounded or weak prey for them to practise on. Yet another thing we would need to duplicate for Tess somehow. I dreaded having to do it – but how else would she learn to survive alone in the bush? Perhaps it was what Papi wanted Rodrigo and Assia to do while I was away, though I told myself Tess was still too young for that lesson.

For the next two Sundays of my stay, I was on the lookout for cheetahs and I was not disappointed. Twice I saw a mother with three small cubs, then another with two subadults following her, though how much success the mothers had out hunting with their boisterous young in tow, sadly, I could not remain to find out. Once I did see a cheetah lying down in the savannah scrub watching her sole cub busily feeding on a kill; when we neared, the cheetah rose and joined her youngster in the feast – perhaps anxious we were there to steal it...

On my last Sunday we were riding out down a wide, dry river bed when I had an uncanny experience. Ten of us in horizontal formation, joking and laughing, pulled up our horses almost simultaneously at a raised hand signal from our leader and listened. Gradually we made out a strange rumbling noise like thunder in the far distance, but the sky was clear and blue. At this, our host shouted to us to get up on to the bank at once. We scrambled up its sides and back a little, and then turned to look at him, in part anxious, in part with curiosity. 'Keep well back from the edge and wait there!' he ordered harshly. And we did. The rumbling grew to a roar, louder and louder, when suddenly we saw it – a wall of water about two metres high, brown, dirty, with branches, even tree trunks, swirling on its crest as it careered down the dry river bed in which we had been riding, and rushed past.

'What was that?' we all shouted, eyes wide.

'That, children,' announced our leader, 'is the spring torrent coming down from mountains after the rains and even after snow has melted on the escarpment far away.'

In fact, I discovered that snow was rare in Namibia but not unknown, hence the sloping roofs of the houses in Windhoek. It was likely that our flash flood – which soon passed, leaving a river not more than thirty centimetres deep – came from recent rain further north.

I was so taken with all I had seen that, greedy for more, when an invitation came to spend a few days with other friends about two hours' drive away, I took it and left the riding course I was on.

Naturally, only cheetahs could have drawn me away. My new hosts had a tame one with three young about the same age as Tess. How could I refuse? And what could I learn? Firstly that their mother cheetah was not house-trained and lived in a stable with the door left open. Their horses had minded very much and another stable had to be built when she gave birth to her first litter. They called her Maya and intended to release her back into the wild – hence not too much domesticity for her or her cubs. But handle them we did – the first time I had touched cubs other than Tess. Maya was tender in her approach to her young and not at all resentful of a new pair of hands holding them; she walked back and forth between them, licking and poking them with her nose. They ran about the stable, which had five loose boxes for them to play in, and the family's Hungarian pointer bitch proved another excellent nanny. When Maya lay down all three cubs came to suckle – they were not yet on solid food and I queried that. My hosts explained that they were going to let Maya and the cubs out into a large enclosure with a few small antelope for her to hunt and show her cubs how. I both did and yet did not want to see this cat-and-mouse display, useful though it might have been, and in the end I left before it began. But I had picked up a number of tips for Tess, including some ideas for toys for her – bicycle tyres and cricket balls were recommended and especially a leather soccer ball that she and the dogs could play with. A year later I heard that Maya and her grown cubs had all been successfully returned to the wild, and that encouraged me a lot.

I returned to my friends' cattle ranch and took part in the final gymkhana. This had always been planned as the closing event of the course and a chance to show the horses we had been training to prospective buyers. Instead of a triumph, I had a bad fall and was told it served me right for having abandoned the course to see more of Namibia's wildlife; that my regular ride, a horse named

Dollar, wanted to teach me a lesson! And that he certainly did. Chastened, I flew home to Maforga and all that awaited me there. It was March; my Tess was now four months old and I was anxious to see how much she had learned in my absence in the hands of Rodrigo and Assia.

CHAPTER V

Since Tess had been taken to hunt only within the fenced jungle area which enclosed our circumambulatory driveway, she could not run off and get lost. At her young age, we all agreed this was the wisest course. These trips into the dense thicket of the jungle around the drive may have been good training for her eventual return to the wild, but she also collected some ticks which I had to pull off her in the same way I pulled them off the dogs. How would she deal with ticks in the wild, I wrote anxiously to Benedita and asked Eduardo on his next visit. Relief when Eduardo told me that if the cheetah is healthy and in good shape – and he would see to it that she was – her parasite load would be low. It was big cats which struggled to find enough food and were generally less healthy, that suffered more – not only from ticks, but also the internal types of parasites. It was during the wet season that we had to be on our guard.

Tess still had some of her ruff running down from the back of her head to her shoulders but by now she was covered in her spots and her legs were longer. She still drank milk from the bottle, and asked for it almost wistfully if I tried to wean her. She was climbing on everything – the furniture indoors (anything fragile was removed) and the low branches of various trees in the garden. She liked heights – the roof of the Land Rover or the canvas-covered trailer from which she could look around and down the great valley and especially over the undulating country of the farm. After inspecting it for a while, she would get up, stretch and go to find a better, cooler resting place under bushes, flopping herself down like a rag doll. Sometimes while sleeping on a shelf or a ledge around the house, she would fall off as she tried to change position, always landing on her feet, but looking deeply embarrassed, turning her head away from any witness as if whistling, pretending it was all intended. In fact, her climbing instincts were becoming a nuisance – she would perch on top of chests of drawers, bookshelves and wardrobes and take a swipe at anyone passing. She would sit so still that any staff in a hurry did not notice her above them at first – then whack! I swear I could see her eyes laughing – though not the swiped victim's!

I decided it might be an idea to make her a proper outdoor playground to climb around instead of letting her clamber about inside the house and so I summoned Joao the farm's carpenter. With the help of Francisco translating, I explained what I wanted and drew a number of diagrams. Joao drew better than I did and soon we had quite a sophisticated plan for a run of obstacles at a height of not less than a metre, some a metre and a half. We reasoned they should all be of a height that she could jump up on with the help of lower steps and they should have flat platforms at the top for sitting or lying on. There was even one with several levels she could choose from – this would become her favourite. The obstacles were to be made out of old packing cases and even some new ones. Papi had established a small plantation of a variety of fast-growing tree ideal for making packing cases for fruit and avocados, and off I went with Joao and Francisco to the warehouse to see what we could find there. The 'bosses' were in Beira for a few days, so we took whatever we thought would be useful – surely they would not want the old, used packing cases – and we were carried away by our enthusiasm.

Joao was a genius – a good carpenter with imagination – and he began to build a super cheetah playground for Tess, who came to watch and practise on the formations as they went up. We wanted it near the house for easy access, and placed it in such a way that the finished arrangement of hurdles covered a large part of the curved front lawn, one of the features of Rosemarie's garden. There were twelve different-shaped obstacles in all, some including old vehicle tyres with a rope running through them and hung ten centimetres above the ground. These Tess would climb through, attack-play with and try to bite. Another was one step up and then another, a leap to the top, down a few steps, then another leap up – it was Tess's Castle and she was enjoying its construction immensely.

'Shall we paint it? asked Francisco, longing to get stuck into a pot of red paint he found. 'No!' I cried – Tess would have paint drying on her paws and between her toes and I would never get it out, or off her coat, and surely turpentine would not be good for her skin, either. That boy had to be watched.

When the playground was finished it had a swing with a seat wide enough for Tess to lie on which hung down from a branch of a jacaranda overlooking the lawn; a series of tyres she could find a way through or climb on top. There were six different 'houses' with extra, higher floors she could climb up on to and a ladder with flat steps which lent against the tall jacaranda where she could lie on a wide platform attached to its lowest branch. The whole was brilliantly devised by Joao and, once we started leaving small pieces of meat on each level and on the ladder's steps, it took no time for Tess to understand she had to find the treat. I could tell she enjoyed herself since she would come and wrapped a forepaw around one of my legs, asking for more. Both 'indoor' and 'outdoor' dogs joined in the hunt for the treats – and what a swipe Tess gave them if they beat her to the little piece of meat. We laughed so much watching her climb on to every level of her Kitty Castle, her claws barely allowing her to hold on to a level before reaching up, her hind legs left struggling.

The next morning I had two surprises. The first was that Eduardo came by to admire Tess's playground and I saw Francisco whispering to him. Tess had used the top platform of one of the landings as a WC. 'Cheetahs like tall, flat places,' said Eduardo, laughing, and I made a mental note to check the tops of the wardrobes in the house…

My next surprise was less amusing – Papi and Rosemarie came home, followed by a smart official car with a little flag fluttering on the bonnet. I had completely forgotten they were bringing the Mayor of Beira and his wife out to the farm for lunch never a bad idea to be friends with the government representatives.

Most of the house staff were engaged on some task on my obstacle course, and none looking too tidy while building and making adjustments, while I had been crawling through the tyres in front of Tess to show her the way – and looked a real mess. The staff fled indoors to try to prepare for the visitors and I was left facing a red-faced father and embarrassed-looking Rosemarie. They must have been praising me generously to their friends and here I was – not the picture of a European young lady our Portuguese guests expected, but extremely dishevelled and grubby, with a bouncy young cheetah not wearing any restraint next to me. The Mayor's wife got straight back in the car when she saw Tess running up to Papi and Rosemarie, and the Mayor blanched. I dashed to grasp Tess by the scruff and sent Francisco for her halter and lead. Tess jumped up on Papi as she usually did and, even at that young age, her front paws reached his chest.

Rosemarie kept her voice low and quiet (always a dangerous sign) and suggested I go inside with Tess to my quarters and change my clothes while they and their guests withdrew to the long terrace. Joao had disappeared along with everyone else. I took Tess into my part of the house – 'by the back way,' said Rosemarie gently – the door leading directly into my bathroom from the kitchen side of the house. I must have been very dirty…

We, the building gang, never thought Rosemarie would mind having Tess's playground on the front lawn. It looked very functional, I thought – there was enough room for it and the lawn was used just for one small tea table in the middle. The fact of its pristine beauty had eluded me. Once clean I joined the guests for lunch and was relieved to see that Benedita had also arrived to be with us. I had received a stern message to leave Tess in my room while our guests were there and I could hear her yowling and scratching on the other side of my door which led into the dining area. Finally Benedita and I went to fetch her, but with her halter, and we kept her well away from the terrified Mayor and his wife. I assured them that cheetahs do not eat humans, but that did little to reassure them. Conversation was stilted and little was eaten.

After we left the table, I stayed away from the others with Tess and as soon as the Mayor and his wife had finished their coffee they left, pleading another engagement in the area. The visit was a fiasco. Papi had hoped to soften the Mayor for some help with a particular project and he had not even dared to raise it. I knew I was in trouble, but I never realised how much. Papi was speechless with rage – I had spoiled his carefully laid plans. Rosemarie was ashamed of her beautiful garden looking like some of the 'abandoned scrapyards in town', she said – and how could I have destroyed her immaculate lawn? Tess and I decided to go for a long walk with Francisco to let them cool off.

That evening Papi said that the obstacle course had to be removed the next day and he hoped that I had not damaged the lawn too badly; that Rosemarie was deeply upset and that I should go to her to apologise. I took Tess with me and when we reached her room – a lovely suite overlooking the escarpment towards Beira – Tess immediately bumped Rosemarie's legs and licked her hand. How could she be cross – she loved Tess and realised I had done it to help amuse 'our' cheetah. She forgave me *but* I had to pretend to Papi that she had given me a good scolding and had then agreed that since the obstacles were up and a success they could stay. Crisis over, we both hugged Tess and one another.

The obstacle course became and remained Tess's favourite amusement, especially since Joao and I kept making additions. The dogs and Tess never seemed to tire of playing hide and seek, finding treats or indulging in a sort of tag, trying to catch one another around the boxes. She enjoyed a tug-of-war using a thick rope, with any of us or with the houseboys.

Often Tess would play football with the dogs, Francisco and I taking part. I would throw the soccer ball into their scrum. Once Tess had it in her mouth, we could do nothing, but as long as we could throw it or kick it, only she could jump high enough to catch it. This infuriated the dogs, especially Calypso, who still occasionally rankled at having been denied my bedroom once Tess came to live with us, although she knew full well she was better off under Rosemarie's tender care.

Another trick Tess had was to use one of her front legs to swipe at the dogs' legs and trip them (or me) up, just as she would do eventually when hunting in the wild. I remember Eduardo telling me that all play among cubs was a preparation for hunting. Tess had no siblings, just me and Daisy, so I watched out for those flashing forelegs – let her practise on the dogs!

Tess always sniffed me when I came back from an outing in town, or when I had been away for a few days – as if I might be someone else. An early piece of advice from Benedita had been that when returning home after an absence I should wear something she knew was a part of me and that she could recognise from sight, which was better than her sense of smell. On the farm I usually wore khaki trousers and a shirt that were indeed familiar, but coming back from church one Sunday, directly after a few days in Umtali, I was surprised to find that Tess low-growled at me as I approached, until she heard my voice. Despite the brilliant long-range horizontal vision that all cheetahs have, she had not recognised me instantly; perhaps I was too close and out of my day character in a blue dress and shoes, hair covered by a hat and sunglasses. In fact I have found that cheetahs do not like sunglasses on people they are with!

To be fair, the Portuguese colonialists, whatever else one might have heard said about them, were very serious about conservation and firm about the restrictions on hunting, as we discovered to our cost. One day during the hunting season in June, I was following my father in the bush, tracking a buffalo that had been wounded by one of our neighbours. While walking through high grass, we failed to notice we were in the middle of a widespread herd of elephants. In their careful, organised societies, old cows which no longer breed take care of the young – these were the potentially bad-tempered 'nannies' or *maridi* I had been warned about. While following the buffalo's tracks we had inadvertently wandered between some elephant calves and their nanny minders.

With a sudden blast of elephant trumpeting, coming from we knew not where, we were charged by an old cow, furious in her rage at our presence near her young charges – which we could not see either. My father, always ice calm in any dangerous situation (I was told this had been the reason for his success in shooting competitions), placed his big rifle on the shoulder of Ravo standing in front of him, aimed carefully and pulled the trigger. The beast fell dead, shot between the eyes. Almost immediately, a second old cow hidden in the tall grass charged from the right-hand side, and this one was even closer. My father calmly shot her as well, and she dropped dead so near us that the ground beneath my feet shook like a small earthquake.

At the time I was totally unaware that the others in our party had fled or climbed trees, but I gloried in the never-ending (taller and taller) tales about my courage, how I was the only one who had not run for safety, climbed a tree, etc. The truth was far simpler – I was totally ossified, rooted to the spot with pure fear and could not move, dared not breathe! I let them talk – why not?

Nor were the horrors of that day yet over. In no time the Portuguese rangers arrived: *two* elephants had been shot and my father had a licence for one! No explanation would do. His guns were seized and his court case would not come up for six months – six months without guns in Africa! (Fortunately Rosemarie had hers at home.) When the case was finally heard, to the relief of us all, the judge agreed that, since the meat on those two old cows had not been worth feeding to our workers and as the beasts had had virtually no tusks, Papi's story of shooting them in self-defence must be true. If not, Rosemarie told me later, Papi might even have gone to jail.

I had developed a special way of calling Tess, a sort of sing-song 'Te-ess, Te-ess' – then she could be sure it was me, her mother, calling. When I drove back from shopping or an expedition somewhere, I would beep a particular rhythm on the Land Rover's horn which she learned to recognise and would come running, with those lovely, bouncing, loping strides. Then a head bump against my legs, a rub of her face on them too, all the while purring loudly and even the occasional high-pitched *aiyhee, aiyhee* – was it cheetah language for 'hello'? It was Benedita who told me that cheetahs purr the loudest when siblings are grooming one another or when they are with their mother. I tape-recorded Tess's loud purring.

Something else which I had to ask Eduardo about, and urgently, was that I found Tess licking mud. When I next saw him he reassured me that this was how a cheetah acquires the minerals it needs. Another strange sight was Tess as a leggy eight-month-old still happily climbing trees, though not tall ones. She got up them well enough, but coming down was less elegant – a bit of a slither, an anxious chirrup or *aiyhee*, a look around – for help, perhaps – then a bit more slide to be mercifully stopped by the support of a fork in the tree. More hesitation, then finally she would let go and continue sliding-running down the trunk, almost flopping down on the ground with outstretched legs, and looking quite embarrassed!

Adult cheetahs are not natural climbers of trees, but Eduardo explained that their change of habitat from the open savannah – where they had more predator enemies, less to hunt and where the grasslands were being used more and more by farmers – to our denser forestation had forced them to learn to climb, despite the limitations of their physique. Those hard pads which give them such traction at speed are not adhesive like those of other climbing animals, and cheetahs are too tall off the ground to slink down on branches. At his previous employment Eduardo had been obliged to deal with the broken bones of young cheetahs that had jumped down from too great a height. If a leg injury did not heal it could spell the end of a cheetah's life.

In the wild, cheetah cubs can depend on their mother to hunt for them and to teach them to hunt from about six months old. But since Tess had no mother to teach her I was very surprised when, at ten months old, she began chirruping to be let out at dawn. For the last two months she had shown signs of wanting to chase prey – mostly quite unsuitably large – but at least it showed she was keen to provide for herself. I began to tape-record her vocalisations to play to Eduardo or Benedita in the hope they could explain them to me.

They told me a great deal, and I have gleaned more over the years. Although I had learned to 'read' Tess's calls, I was unaware of the rest. I knew that cheetahs did not make sounds like the lion, leopard or tiger. They have unique calls for communicating with their mother, their siblings and their own cubs. Since they do not live in social groups, they do not need as large a vocabulary as lions, but they have a very distinct language nonetheless. The first sound I heard from Tess is known as *yipping* – a short, high-pitched yelp when she wanted to know where I was or where to find her nanny, Ridgeback Daisy. Had she had siblings, they would have *yipped* or *ayipped* to call each other. This is the sound I have described as imitating bird calls and is also referred to as *chirping* or *chirruping*. I have heard small cubs use this when faced with an unfamiliar adult cheetah through the wire netting of their separate 'nurseries' at the Kapama Centre in South Africa. Adult cheetahs also yip, and very loudly if afraid.

Then there is the *churr*, a sort of stuttering bark cheetahs make when they meet socially. It is a rather cosy sound which mothers make to call their cubs to suckle. At Kapama, I was once filming the first cub of a litter to leave its birthing hut and it approached the wire netting dividing its nursery from that of a very pregnant cheetah on the other side. On seeing the little cub, the pregnant cheetah churred to show interest and repeated the sound even more loudly when the cub's mother came out to join them. I have not heard males churr, but am told they do it when meeting females, and the ladies tend to churr when anxious about males nearby.

More serious is the *yowl*, which indicates a threat, a long drawn-out moan to warn of danger, especially when a predator approaches a cheetah's cubs. Cheetahs also hiss, spit, growl and, of course, purr.

If I did not react to any one of Tess's various vocalisations, she would stamp one of her forelegs most insistently. *Thump! thump!* Stamping the foreleg while sitting upright is a much used sign of displeasure in cheetahs and one of which to be wary – it was never a sign that she wanted to play!

When Tess began churring in the early morning while I was still asleep, it could only mean she wanted to go hunting – it was much easier for her to ask to go out at the end of the day or to find an open door. After some discussion at home, I asked Joao to devise a sort of cat flap so that she could go out in the early mornings without letting other animals come in. This was quite a challenge for him, but he succeeded in devising a sort of chicane which the rapidly growing cheetah understood how to manage surprisingly easily. The unattractive and convoluted but useful exit was erected to lead out of my dressing-room window, visible from my bed. Of course I worried about a snake getting in through it, but Antonio the cook promised he had asked his brother to 'cast a spell over the chicane so there would be no unwanted visitors'. Having seen what magic Antonio's brother was capable of producing, I was somewhat reassured.

I knew that cheetahs were diurnal, hunting in daylight, unlike the other big cats, and as yet Tess had not asked to go out towards the end of the day, which, along with the early morning, is their preferred hunting time. In the evening, she still liked to sit with us and various dogs on the terrace, stretch out to her full length, yawn, showing her magnificent teeth, and doze. When the nights became cooler in the winter months, Tess, who had been allowed the freedom of the house at about six months, would take the prime position in front of the large open fire, surrounded by Daisy and the indoor dogs, and snore – a soft, gentle sound, I thought, but which Papi swore could 'wake the dead', as he would delight in exclaiming, rustling his papers while reading in the evenings. Papi never made a fuss over Tess, but I could see how attached to her he was – despite his disapproval of taming wild animals!

One day Tess came to me with a sore eye – closed, weeping with infection and swollen around the edge. It must have come up during the night and of course I panicked: 'Papi, help!' He packed us both into the Land Rover and we headed for town and Eduardo's clinic. Thankfully he was there and Tess knew him well enough not to hiss, spit or bite him. He quickly saw that the problem was a thorn wedged in the edge of her lower eyelid and said he would have to sedate her to extract it. Apparently this happens quite often to cheetahs in denser undergrowth or when the grass is long after rain. I stayed with Tess the whole time while Eduardo shaved around the eye, removed the thorn and stitched the lid. I have since seen another beloved hand-reared cheetah at Kapama with a similar wound caused by a thorn and fortunately he, too, was well treated and recovered fully.

When Tess came around, I was still there, anxious Mother Cat. Papi had gone to shop in town and when he came back he had eaten lunch with a friend he met and thought me very silly to have made such a fuss and stayed by her as if she were my child. Young as I was, Tess was indeed my first experience of motherhood after all. Eduardo could not stress often enough how lucky Tess had been not to have had worse injuries or stomach problems during her young life.

By now, all the house staff and our principal outdoor staff were totally accustomed to Tess and her ways and returned her affection – except perhaps the kitchen staff, aware that she was always trying to slip into the kitchen yard and sneak a treat. So far we had not had an incident with a snake, although she had become aware of the tenants living over my bedroom ceiling.

They were our 'indoor snakes' – but these we liked. Often when I lay in bed at night, I would hear the pitter-patter of tiny feet scurrying along the floor of the ceiling above me in the attic. This was then followed by a slow slide/slither, pause, slide/slither as a house python made its way after a rat. Both rats and pythons remained in the attic as far as I know, because I never saw either but I always heard them. The snakes had to eat to live and the rats would breed the snakes' future dinners – I guess while they ate our own scraps by or in the bins. Tess could hear these activities and often sat up, ears cocked, issuing a low growl.

In the evenings, the house was beautifully lit with pressure lamps, which one member of the staff spent all day pumping so that we could see and read by them. They were made from antique Chinese tea caddies with old-fashioned hexagonal parchment shades over them, and will always remind me of African nights, still but for their gentle hiss, the birds and the occasional calls of lions. Once they had been turned out these lamps could not be re-lit by us. Any movement afterwards in the dark had to be lit by a candle or a torch, both of which I kept by my bed. One night when I rose to visit the bathroom, as usual guided by my torch, I took the prescribed precaution of shining it about, checking for scorpions or whatever, and, of course, Tess sleeping by my bed. When I climbed over her, she rolled to her other side without waking. Reaching the bathroom, I had quite a shock. Within the bowl of the WC, half in the water and flat against the cool porcelain, there lay curled – a black mamba.

I dropped the lid and ran through the house, Tess awake now and by my side, to the other end where my father slept. I shook him awake without ceremony. 'Papi! Papi! A snake, a black one, a black mamba in my loo! Do something!' He was so amused at my fright and at the sight of Tess by my side like a guard dog that he almost laughed me into real anger.

'Kill it! Kill it!' I almost screamed at him, shaking. 'I will not have snakes lurking in my loo waiting to bite me.'

'And that is why I taught you to always have a torch and snake-bite antidote in your bedroom and to wear a belt with it when you go outside,' he laughed.

'And what about Tess?' I cried.

'Well, I doubt she will use your loo!'

I know I cried as much out of fear for Tess as for myself. I will never forget how Papi hugged me and told me I could use his bathroom while he went to deal with the snake. I kept Tess with me just in case and when he came back, all smiles, he said: 'Problem dealt with. Now go back to bed.' If he said so, I knew it was true, and Tess and I went back to my room – she, happily, none the wiser. But how had the snake got into my bathroom? I learned then that they always managed to get in where they wanted…

Nestling in subtropical, damp East Africa, about 180 kilometres from the coast, Maforga was a haven for snakes – they were everywhere, and poisonous. One I particularly disliked was the spitting cobra which would grow to over two metres long and as fat as a salami, the folds of skin on either side of its head extended when it was about to spit. It would carefully aim at the eyes of its prey, which then wandered blindly towards it. The snake would then bite and hang on until its victim was dead. When faced with a much larger animal, the spitting was used more as a deterrent, as if to say, 'Go away.' This type of cobra ate smaller animals, nothing like the size of our dogs. But on a number of occasions the dogs staggered home with the snake's sticky excretions covering their eyes and, although I never saw the snake actually spitting, I did not want to either. The easiest way for us to remove the sticky stuff was warm milk, which, naturally, Tess would try to steal as I washed the poor dogs' eyes with it.

As Tess grew, she often left by the chicane in my window at first light and occasionally returned with an unsolicited present, not always dead, which she placed by my bed. On rising I would find it, barely alive – a lizard, mouse, rat, gecko, baby bird or rabbit, among other small creatures. I realised the killing of it was my perquisite – ugh! I had to shout for someone to remove the wounded creature and surreptitiously put it out of its misery. And, of course, I would fuss over Tess, feigning gratitude for her gift.

As she became more amenable to our lives, flopping about with the indoor dogs, following me around the house and garden, I began to take her in Rosemarie's car with me to do errands. All the locals knew about my cheetah and that, if left alone, she would not hurt them. I did put on her harness and kept her on a lead in our small town, but I enjoyed taking her shopping with me and to the Post Office, where she was a great favourite. When Papi heard of these little excursions he fussed. 'Will you learn she is not a dog or a house pet – she must go back into the wild.' But I did take her visiting sometimes to the neighbours – showing off I guess – but also because she was such delightful company and funny. Visiting a young couple, charming neighbours, she picked up a rather nice small straw hat left on a table one Sunday after church and would not let it go. She sat with it hanging from her mouth in the strangest way, dark blue straw with flowers and cherries drooping down.

Tess loved flowers, especially when their heads moved in the breeze, she would catch them and pull them up out of the flower beds around the house – and anyone else's as well. Not popular with Rosemarie. And she loved oranges. I would walk with her between the long rows of citrus trees, blossom on them at the same time as fruit in that unique climate, the scent delicious, the ground kept swept clean of grass and leaves. Often there were fallen oranges under the trees that had not yet been cleared and these were a favourite toy – we called it playing Orange Football. Tess would clip and hook the fruit, rolling it along, our workers kicking it back to her. Then the ridgebacks would join in and, since Tess was now almost as big as they were, it became quite a tussle. I had to watch carefully so that the game did not descend into a fight for dominance, but Tess usually gave up before they did, out of breath. I noticed how Daisy would always play on Tess's side, not on that of her boys'.

Tess was about ten months old when Eduardo suggested that he should join Assia and Rodrigo in training Tess to hunt. She could never be returned to the wild if she could not hunt and this was the aim of us all. Well, I knew it had to be. They were all aware I was rather squeamish about this procedure, since an animal would have to be maimed for Tess to be able to catch and kill it at this age. Therefore it was decided that I should go away and undertake another trip within Africa – there was much to see and I was not to interrupt Tess's training with my queasy outbursts.

I flew south to join family friends in Cape Town, intending to remain for a couple of weeks. Cape Town dazzled me. That astonishing flat-topped mountain I was challenged to climb by the young members of my host's family – and the views. We visited several vineyards in the Cape area of Stellenbosch and tried different vintages; went to a game park in the Kruger, where I was sad not to see cheetahs, though some leopards made up for it. I met a number of amiable young people, especially equestrians, and rode out with them on a farm near Cape Town. I visited the glorious seaside town of Hermanus and swam every day in the surf. In fact, I was having such a happy time that I wanted to stay a little longer by the sea before returning to the farm for Christmas. 'Why not?' echoed my young hosts. That was when I learned that an air ticket could be returned to a travel agent for cash – and I would have funds to remain for more play. So this I did.

Two weeks later, at the beginning of December, I realised I had to make plans for my trip home and asked around for an inexpensive way to travel – I had spent much of my airfare bonus already. It transpired that the cheapest way to complete the long journey back to Mozambique, nearly three thousand kilometres, was by bus. Fine – I like buses. But it would take almost three weeks – well, I would have to hurry and make plans right away. At the travel agent I made enquiries and discovered that there was indeed a regular bus service, but available only to Africans and 'Coloureds' – the designation given in those days to people in the Cape of mixed blood. It was 1962 and I was new to the strictures of apartheid then in force. With the help of my young friends, I decided I would take that bus. But for a tall, blonde, green-eyed European girl to pass as a mixed-race local, some adjustments would have to be made.

It was all such a game at the time – if I had to be of mixed race to be able to take the bus, then that is what I would become. I washed a black dye into my long blonde hair, and lay in the sun until I was as brown as I could be. (I am suffering for that now!) Then, accompanied by the African housemaid of my hosts, who had no idea what I was doing, I approached a different travel agency and paid for a bus ticket to Mozambique. To add to my disguise, I bought a grey-painted tin trunk which I was assured was the luggage of choice of my fellow travellers and stocked up on rations for the trip. I intended to write the story of my journey and this gave me a goal. Preparing for my adventure thrilled me and I had no concept of any problems. Politically incorrect as it would rightly appear today, that was the attitude prevalent in 'white man's Africa' in the early 1960s.

I booked my place to sit in the very front of the bus on a long bench which held the driver and could have seated four passengers, but I was the only one. I sensed my father and stepmother would not be in favour of this new arrangement and swore my guardians in Cape Town to secrecy.

Naturally, I asked about sleeping arrangements and was told that most of the passengers slept on the bus, which stopped for about six or seven hours each night for the needs of the driver; others slept by the side of the road with a little fire and much chatting and laughter. I bought a sleeping bag and asked if I could lie down along the full length of the front seat. The driver agreed. My sleeping bag zipped up to my chin for the chilly nights, and I had no thoughts of any possible risk, probably due to the innocence of youth and my solid faith in humankind. Happily, this would be justified.

As well as a few changes of basic clothing, tins of food and packets of cereal, my grey tin trunk, closed with a huge padlock, stocked a large quantity of lavatory paper. I had been warned by my giggling friends, curious as to how I would manage, that the bathroom facilities would be minimal at the gas stations. Being a practical girl by nature, I was not fazed. I travelled with a small folding umbrella for protection more from the sun than from rain, but, then, I would not mind the sunshine in my new incarnation, would I? I was informed that the bus usually made a number of 'pit stops' on the road for the passengers, who quickly disappeared into the bush. That did not appeal to me at all – snakes, scorpions, biting insects... No, I had a different plan. I knew the road would be dirt and not tarmac, therefore I would walk back a short distance along the way we had come, carrying my folding umbrella and a roll of loo paper under my arm. I would open the umbrella, squat down behind it and, like the good cat I was, bury the paper etc. neatly; then I would dress, rise, close the umbrella and return to the bus. I practised this at my friends' house a number of times just to be sure my plan would work – and it did.

What about washing? Whenever the bus stopped at a petrol station, there were facilities, but none of them looked remotely inviting. But there was always a hose available for the vehicles and, since it was December and the days were hot, I had no hesitation in hosing myself down fully clothed from the top of my head to my toes. That would have to do. The sun dried me long before the bus was ready to leave.

It was at one of these petrol stops that I noticed a small brown monkey on a long thin chain sitting on a wooden post, the property of the station manager. I went to stroke it, which it seemed to enjoy – and then suddenly, it bit my finger, the middle joint on my right hand   not too hard, but it drew a little blood. Never mind, I sucked my finger and forgot about it as we boarded our bus and travelled on.

The next morning I woke to a throbbing ache in my hand, arm and armpit as well as a woozy, feverish feeling. I showed my hand and arm to the driver – a red line travelling up the inside from my swollen finger to my armpit.

'You need doctor,' he told me and then showed my arm to the passengers, who all looked horrified and mumbled among themselves, obviously concerned. By this time I had been travelling on the bus for about ten days and knew many of the other passengers, as well as their chickens and goats. These fellow travellers had become my friends: they had fed me after my rations ran out and I had shared mine with them. Their faces looked anxious and after much mumbling they agreed I needed a doctor. By then my fever was making me delirious and I, too, agreed and mumbled 'doctor' along with them.

Some time later, we turned off the main road and bumped along a rough track until we came to a village. 'Doctor,' said the nervous driver. I was lifted down from the bus, too feverish to ask or to care what was going on. As we were soon surrounded by the villagers, after much animated discussion I was carried into a hut. There I stayed for the next two days, floating in and out of consciousness as someone tended to me. Dreamily, I was aware of a woman, a silently moving slender shape in red, perhaps an angel…

When I could hear, think, see more clearly, I realised that the bus and all the passengers had remained with me for two whole days and nights; that they had been afraid I might die; that perhaps I might have important connections and if I died that could prove difficult for them. Then I met my doctor and was told he was a well-known local witch doctor! He beamed at me and gave me a small pouch of something soft wrapped in a thin skin like a sausage. 'Give to your home doctor,' he kept repeating, for although most people spoke English in Southern Rhodesia, as it was then, not all the country people were fluent. I had nothing to give him but smiled and thanked him as best I could, holding both his hands in mine, aware that he may well have saved me from dying. The slender shape in red was his wife, and I thanked her as well.

Still wobbly on my feet, I was helped back into the bus, but knew my fever had broken and passed. For a while I just sat silently, the curious object of attention from my fellow passengers, who came now and then to stroke or pat me like a much loved dog. I just smiled and nodded in gratitude as I wondered at the courage and generosity of these good people whom I hardly knew. If I had died in those pre-independence days, the consequences for them might have been quite serious – but I only realised that much later.

When I arrived home I did give the strange 'med'sin' to our local clinic. After they analysed it they told me it had been made from plants and other ingredients which formed the basis of a natural antibiotic. The astonishing extent of what Africa's witch doctors knew I would come to experience with gratitude and admiration on a number of occasions during my visits to the continent.

On we travelled and I healed, taking more interest in my surroundings. Sitting at the front of the bus, I was cradling the map and following our route when I saw, writ in small print, the word 'Zimbabwe'. The country now known as Zimbabwe was called Southern Rhodesia until 1980, and at this time that name would not have been familiar to anyone but a keen student of archaeology. However, at school I had read all about the discovery of the remarkable ruins of Zimbabwe, and the idea that I was passing near them excited me. I begged the driver to stop when we reached the ruins, but he just shook his head – the bus had lost so much time on my account already that he feared he might lose his job if we did not press on. I begged, I pleaded, until finally he told me we would reach the town after dark, that the bus would only be permitted to stop on its outskirts, and that he had to drive on at six in the morning. I would have to rise at dawn, see the ruins and join the bus by six or it would leave without me.

At that time, no one seemed sure who had built this city, using a type of granite then unknown in the area and a form of drystone walling, also not a local technique. Had the stone been floated down the river from elsewhere? On rafts, perhaps, just as the Egyptians had moved their obelisks from their quarries in Aswan? It was a mystery aching to be solved by a keen young student like me! I had seen pictures and read that the ruins were of a city abandoned in the Middle Ages, the walls no longer any higher than about two metres. Certainly some of the building stones had been taken and used by others for a different purpose. But what remained looked fascinating enough to draw me.

As we drove through the town I saw a red neon sign 'Hotel' and asked to be let off there. With my trunk kindly carried in for me, I waved to my friends on the bus, promising to see them in the morning. The elderly lady at the reception desk scrutinised me as I asked for a room with a bath. I told her I had no money but that 'my father would pay' (and, by the way, he did). No questions were asked – 'That's all right, then,' was all she said – and she led me to a perfectly clean room with a comfortable-looking bed, clean sheets and a shower cabinet.

Oh the joy of that shower after ten days without proper washing: the warm water, the basic soap I used on my hair as well as my travel-stained self. Nor will I forget my shock as I saw the black water running down my body onto the floor of the cabinet – my hair! No matter – with a wet ponytail and clean clothes I went to find dinner, a drink and the pleasure of eating sitting at a table. As if that was not enough, tomorrow I would see those magnificent ruins – a whole mysterious city complex. My cup of expectations was full. That is, until I entered the Saloon Bar and saw, to my amazement, some thirty young men standing around talking and holding drinks; blond, bronzed, blue-eyed, all in starched khaki shorts and shirts, Boy Scout belts, long white socks and walking shoes. In this tiny town, one short street with buildings only on either side – who were they? And their eyes asked – who was I?

It was not long before we exchanged information. They were all farmers who were also part-time Special Police to be called up in case of any trouble. Tomorrow, they told me, 14 December 1962, was Election Day. Election Day? Yes, a General Election for seats in the Southern Rhodesian Parliament. It was something I knew little about except that 'Ian Smith' and 'Rhodesian Front Party' were the names being bandied about energetically during the intense discussions taking place around me. Only much later did I understand what those elections had been about and the emergence into power of both the man and the party, which were to retain white rule in Rhodesia for another fifteen years.

My arrival stopped the young men's earnest discussions. They turned to me and asked politely what I was doing there, European seventeen-year-old that I clearly was?

'Oh, I'm getting up early before my bus leaves to view the wonderful ruins of ancient Zimbabwe,' I answered brightly.

This was met with blank looks all round. Finally, someone said quietly, 'But they're not here, you know.'

I was shocked. I had been planning, looking forward to this discovery, studying the bus's route. Wasn't this Zimbabwe Town? Patient sighing — *Yes, but the ruins are about half an hour from here and not in the direction you are travelling.* I must have been close to tears because a kind young man came up with an idea. We had all eaten our dinner by then and had a few drinks, so his suggestion did not sound as outrageous as perhaps it was.

'Tonight there is a full moon, and by the light of our December full moon you can see an ant walking on stones!' he declared with a flourish. 'Why don't we all go now to the ruins?'

To shouts of 'Hooray! Yes! Good idea!', off we went in a convoy of cars. It never occurred to me this was perhaps *not* a good or safe idea, because it seemed the perfect solution. The young men were well-behaved and treated me as an honoured guest.

And that is how I saw the ruins of Great Zimbabwe by the light of December's full moon, sitting huge and still low in the sky, and yes, I swear I could have seen an ant crawling on a stone, the moonlight was so bright and clear. I noticed the strange curved double wall on one side of the city and the even stranger narrow tower, its purpose unknown: I sketched them later when I was back in my room. My escorts and I exchanged some addresses and one or two wrote, but I never saw any of them again.

Then, about ten years ago, I was visiting Botswana with my husband, writing about the Okavango Delta for the *Orient Express* magazine. One evening, sitting around the campfire in this beautiful location, we were talking to the guides about the plans for the next day's outing on the water, when one of them asked me politely whether I had ever visited the ruins of Great Zimbabwe? Yes, I told him, I had, long ago. Had I, by any chance, been there in 1962 at the time of the famous election which divided the country? *He had been one of the farmers/Special Police who had escorted me in the convoy to view the ruins by the light of the full moon.* How small the world can be. Some forty years later, there he was working in an Okavango safari camp, earning money to keep his parents in their Zimbabwe home; they felt too old to move to England. Like so many others, their farm had been taken from them, but they wanted to die in the land in which they had been born and where they had raised their own families. We had heard a number of similar tragic stories.

Just then there was a commotion as an elephant ran into the camp scattering us. His goal was the ripe fruit on a tall marula tree in the middle of our dining area! Nor was that the end of our adventures in that camp. On another day while we were there a leopard wandered into one of the tents and was only tempted to leave with some difficulty. Then a week after we left, a hippo

surfaced in the delta and bit a dugout canoe into three pieces —
his mouth was so large it contained the centre piece and left one
third on either side. Tragically, the canoe was being paddled by a
honeymoon couple and the young wife was killed.

After my view of the ruins of Great Zimbabwe, the rest of my
bus journey home to Mozambique was uneventful. I had been
right to fear my father's anger when he discovered how I had
travelled, but once he had heard of my illness after the monkey
bite, I was reluctantly forgiven.

CHAPTER VI

Arriving back on the farm after my stay in the south, I was enchanted with the way Tess had progressed. She was growing into a splendid creature and I heard all about the many stages of her development during my absence. Christmas came and decorating the tree was the source of much merriment. At just over a year old, Tess was now able to pull down decorations from quite a height. There was no alternative – we only decorated the top quarter and no more lametta! There were more decorations on the floor than on the tree – it was a wreck. Nor could I set up the tabernacle – papier mâché Joseph and donkey were shredded in no time. When the plantation workers came to the front lawn to receive their gifts (a small cake each, which they liked and which had been bought for them in Beira, and a Christmas bonus), we stood on the front steps as a family, Tess sitting upright by my side, the dogs as well, while Papi made a short speech. If only there had been a photographer!

This was followed by another presentation to the house staff and then we received their gifts – they had baked their own-recipe biscuits for us, and had made another offering for Tess. This was something I was told she liked – a meat loaf made from wild hare! She took it gently, as she did all food given to her by hand, but it did not last long… then she lay down near the dining table and slept.

Guests from Europe came for New Year and despite the heat they enjoyed a safari with Papi and Rosemarie – and I was allowed to bring Tess and Francisco. This would be her first time in real bush, not on the farm, and, although firmly attached to the strong lead on her harness, she was very energetic and interested in the world around her.

The drive out to our chosen and favourite safari site was full of excitement. Tess, initially sitting between Papi and me in the Land Rover, soon moved to my lap and then pushed me aside so she could have the window seat. I dared not open the window more than a couple of inches and she stuck her nose to the open part, making her strange, deep, rumbling noises with an occasional high-pitched *ihn-ihn* and chirruping. She was happy. And since we did not run over a snake this time, I was confident about our dinner.

It was decided that I would share my tent with Tess, who could sleep in the lobby outside my sleeping area, firmly tethered by her halter, although with enough slack to come and lie by my bed if she wanted. She never wore her halter indoors on the farm, so this seemed very strange to her, as if she were about to be taken out, and at first she was confused and paced about. When she was a tiny cub, I had always sung little nursery songs to her – silly, I know, but what else? Opera? So I tried these again and they seemed to calm her. Not only were her surroundings quite new, but also the sounds – so much louder in the bush than at the farm – and she stirred and sat up often. Not much sleep for this Cheetah Mother that night.

We all rose before dawn and set off after breakfast. I had Francisco by my side, while Tess would pull away from me if she saw something to hunt. We had brought and given her a fresh kill from the day before so that she was not hungry in the morning, and we hoped that would discourage her from wanting to chase prey.

There followed an extraordinary two days, taking a subadult cheetah on a photo safari... Papi had taken the precaution of bringing not only Ravo but also Assia and Rodrigo with us. They told me how, in my absence, Tess had learned to hunt – spot, stalk, run and choke – as if she had never been brought up by human hand. She crouched the moment anything came into sight, did not move a hair, and watched intently again and again. The hunters did not want to upset me with details, but I heard that on three occasions they had brought her slightly lamed animals to catch and kill and she did what a cheetah has to do. More I did not ask, nor was I told.

What a schoolgirl I still was – now I would be much more matter of fact. Nature is cruel by definition and carnivores must eat meat to live. Unlike a fox, a cheetah will kill only what it needs for sustenance.

Ours was a watching safari – no shooting, as the visitors were not hunters – so a perfect opportunity to show Tess the bush, especially around Gorongosa, where one day I would have to release her. 'She should become acquainted with the area,' said Papi, 'and come here often. It will be her real home.' My heart sank whenever he spoke like that.

We were fortunate to see quite a lot of game – wildebeest, impala, warthogs. These Tess sat upright for and I held her halter firmly. We saw some elephants with two little ones, plenty of zebras and also several giraffe.

And on the last day, several fine buffaloes. Our guests were pleased; much merriment around the campfire eating bushbuck and impala killed by Ravo – Assia and Rodrigo, who would normally have been shooting our food, had their hands full with Tess, but she enjoyed eating some of the game as well. I was fascinated to see that when she began to eat from a carcass, she would sit with her front legs tucked under her. I expected her to hold the carcass but she just pushed her nose and mouth in!

Not long after this first safari for Tess, Eduardo, ever attentive and cheerful about what he saw as *his* great feline charge, came to tell me it was time we taught Tess to run.

'Teach her to run? Surely she knows how to do that?'

'But we do not know how far and how well – let us have her run alongside the Land Rover to find out.'

In fact we used a pick-up truck and had Francisco squat in the back with a supply of fresh antelope meat cut into strips and tied to lengths of string about five or six metres long. His job was to throw a piece attached to string from the pick-up out towards Tess, who was held by Assia, to tempt her with it. Once she showed interest and made to play with it, I would drive off slowly to see if she tried to chase the meat. At first I was too slow and she pounced on it at once and ate it; at other times I was too fast and she lost interest and sat down. But with trial and error, and deprived of her usual breakfast, she was hungry enough to chase the meat bouncing along behind the vehicle.

I kept her in my rear-view mirror all the time – when she slowed, so did I; when she was catching up too quickly, I accelerated. By not going on with the game for too long at one stretch, we prevented her from becoming bored – or from eating her fill – and I managed to increase the distances she would run, and the size of the prize. It was a great game for her, and exciting for us to see how fast she was becoming. For fear of turning over the pick-up, I did not dare twist and turn, as an antelope would have done had she been chasing prey in the wild, and there was not much width on the driveway either, but when I clocked her at eighty kilometres an hour we were confident she could run fast and well. Some days I would let Francisco drive the pick-up, which he loved doing, and Antonio the cook would take his place throwing the meat on the string. Soon it would be time for her to go out with Assia and Rodrigo, hunting the smaller antelope – duiker, steenbok, sunni, oribi – which we had on our land. I was warned she would not succeed at first, and I would have to wait patiently.

At this time, Papi and I, accompanied by Rodrigo and Assia, who were both thrilled at their involvement with Tess, would go for walks – more like hikes – around the concession where Papi hunted. Although Tess had been with us on our New Year's safari, at first we did not plan to remain overnight and would leave the house very early in the morning. With the dawn, Tess was sitting alongside me by the window in front, open wider this time, and I next to Papi driving the Land Rover. She was incredibly alert as we drove along, more so than on our first visit to our safari area, her 180-degree eyesight scanning the side of the dirt road. I was so close to her, with my arm around her as well, that I could feel her stiffen when she saw potential game, but she was already wearing her halter and lead – I could not afford an escape and chase if we stopped and I opened the car door.

When we arrived at our prearranged location, we would walk together, the four of us and Tess, and stop when she stopped, her eyesight better than ours. Binoculars would be raised until we saw what she had spotted – though I am sure Rodrigo and Assia saw almost as well as she did. Cheetahs have poor colour vision and rely on their prey's movement. Should the prey blend with its surroundings and lie still, a cheetah could miss it altogether – such as a young antelope hidden by its mother.

Holding on to Tess's lead, I could feel her tremble slightly, but the object of the exercise was to acquaint her with the open savannah – our own open territory was cultivated land and although antelope sometimes strayed on to it from the denser woodland to nibble at the maize or other crops, what she saw next to the national park was the real world she would inhabit one day. My heart was always torn in two – happy for her future and miserable for mine without her – but eventually 'reason would win over sentiment', as Papi would say.

After several twice-weekly daytime visits to our hunting area, we began to stay overnight, Tess always sleeping by my camp bed, but sharp and alert at dawn, when we would take her out for a long walk, still on the extended lead. She sniffed at everything – our walks were slow – and when she saw potential prey or enemies, she would flatten and so would we. If her tail wagged from side to side, I knew she wanted to hunt. If she did not move, I knew she saw an enemy. On one walk we came across a male lion with four females and their young and we had to back off slowly so as not to draw their attention. Cheetahs are easy prey for lions and if they attacked us all at once… ? We were three hunters and I had a gun as well, but Francisco, who was with us that day, may well have been up a tree in seconds, even with his trusty panga, rather than holding Tess if I gave him her lead while I fired.

After that walk, Papi would not risk Tess meeting lions again and we used the Land Rover to look for game, with her sitting safely beside me and the open window. She loved these outings and whenever I rose before dawn she knew we were going into the bush.

With Tess being well minded by Rodrigo and Assia, who were taking her out hunting with them almost daily, I was engaged in thrilling work at my desk. From all over the world, more and more replies to the many missives I had sent out in every direction were coming back to me, with answers to my questions about the cheetah in history.

I wanted to know their earliest background: who, in earlier times, had tamed, befriended and used cheetahs and how. I was surprised to discover that cheetahs are known to have been in Mesopotamia during Assyrian times (from say 2500BC) before spreading from there to Persia and Central Asia.

The Ancient Egyptians were the first recorded civilisation to have kept cheetahs as pets and hunting companions, since at least 1550BC. The Hittites, their contemporaries in Anatolia (modern Turkey), had mounted their principal goddess on a cheetah.

The conclusion drawn by many sources is that cheetahs have been used for hunting since quite early times, but that the activity was restricted to small and privileged communities – royal families and their adherents – and was therefore not visible to the world at large. Only with the advent of Islam in the seventh century did it become more widespread. There was misperception in terminology as well – many confused the leopard with the cheetah, though the leopard was dangerous to humans whereas the cheetah was not.

Papi and I had already discussed the Egyptians on our journey from Johannesburg to Maforga, but since then I had read more about their relationship with cheetahs. The Pharaohs believed that this fastest of land animals would carry away their spirits to the Afterlife in death. Illustrations on the walls of Pharaonic temples depicted cheetahs with human heads trampling down evil. Further, it is well recorded that Egyptian Pharaohs sent expeditions to the 'Land of Punt' near the Horn of Africa (modern Ethiopia and Somalia) and brought back what they called 'panthers', though their portrayal on tombs, the distinctive tear stripes on their faces, mark them clearly as having been cheetahs. There are a number of other illustrations which show cheetahs, a symbol of elegance for thousands of years, being led on collars and leashes, labelled 'panthers of the north'. Cheetah motifs were also found in Tutankhamen's tomb, forming all four bedposts of a cane bed. All those represented look calm and tame.

It was the Egyptians who first noted the malleable character of the cheetah, recognising it as easy to tame, and they passed the culture of keeping cheetahs as pets and for hunting on to the Persians, long before the arrival of the Mughals in the sixteenth century.

A number of sources maintain that Persia had a native population of cheetahs and a culture of hunting with them, a tradition dating from pre-Islamic times. In the *Shah Nemah*, the tenth-century epic of the Persian kings by the great poet Ferdowsi, there is a story of the Sassanid Emperor Bahram Gur hunting with a cheetah. Another chronicle from the thirteenth century but based on an earlier tradition recounts tales of a seventh-century Sassanid Emperor, Yazdagird, dedicated to hunting with falcons and cheetahs. Despite these accounts, scholars have yet to find tangible evidence of coursing with cheetahs in Persia or anywhere else in the Middle Eastern area at that time. But there seems no doubt that cheetah hunting became both visible and popular and spread to both Muslim and non-Muslim courts from the seventh century.

Fundamentally a gentle and friendly creature, the cheetah feels at home almost anywhere. Its essentially temperate character and acceptance of human domination made it ideal to use as a 'hunting dog' and a royal pet, not only by the Egyptians and the Persians but also by the Cretans, Ancient Greeks and Etruscans. Later, cheetahs would be presented as gifts for the royal menageries in Greece, France and Italy.

As early as the fifth century, cheetahs were used for sport in Italy, then later in Russia, Syria, Palestine, Ethiopia and China.

They were known all over the great Mongol/Chinese Empire with depictions of them on Tang tombs from the seventh century, including that of Li Xian, the heir-apparent Prince of Yung. There is another picture in the tomb of Li Zhongrun (682–701) showing a cheetah tethered to a hunter on foot.

The popularity of cheetahs or 'hunting cats' lasted throughout the Tang dynasty, but with the fall of that family their use declined in most of China. A Song envoy at the Qitan court in 1020 reported seeing three tame 'leopards' riding on horseback with their handlers out on a hunt. We also know that a Turkic people called the Uyghurs presented cheetahs to the Liao court in northeastern China/Mongolia around the eleventh century.

In the early decades of the eighth century, faced with Arab military pressure, the non-Muslim rulers of Turkestan appealed to Tang China for support. The embassy from Turkestan included hunting cats (as well as their keepers) in their tribute missions, assuming that these would be accepted with such favour as to guarantee military aid. The Chinese were already devoted to hunting and were receiving cheetahs from all over the western region, adding a new variant to their passion for the sport. The receipt of such numbers of hunting cats gave the Chinese the impression that hunting with cheetahs was the norm among all international courts of stature. There was always peer pressure in international royal display of every kind – accommodation, festivities and particularly 'the chase'. Great rulers were invariably drawn to something new in the hunt and cheetahs provided that novelty.

Not until the thirteenth century did hunting cats become popular again in the East and this was under Mongolian auspices. Cheetahs were presented to the Mongols in 1220 when the city of Bokhara surrendered to them. We know that the successors to Genghis Khan were attracted to the sport of hunting with cheetahs, although we have not yet found any proof that he himself indulged in it. But the Flemish-Franciscan missionary William of Rubruck spent three years visiting the courts of the Great Khans and left extensive descriptions of their lifestyle. In Karakorum, capital of Genghis Khan's empire, William met the envoys of an Indian potentate who 'brought ten greyhounds and eight leopards who had been taught to sit on a horse's back'. He must have meant cheetahs, since no leopard could have been trained then (or now) to do that. The great Italian explorer Marco Polo, travelling in China during the reign of Genghis's grandson Kublai Khan, mentions cheetahs among the cats stationed at the court of Xanadu – Kublai Khan is said to have kept hundreds of them.

Also in the thirteenth century, other envoys from Persia and the great Sultan Abu Said Mirza of the Timurid dynasty, which covered the area of the 'stans', sent shipments of lions, tigers and leopards (most probably cheetahs) to the ruling Yuan dynasty of China.

All this made me wonder where the cheetahs had come from. Although they had been known in Persia since the time of Alexander the Great, that country's rulers and those of the Golden Horde were deadly rivals, and so it is unlikely Persia was the source of their cheetahs. However, the Great Khan of the Golden Horde, Ozbek, who was active in the Near East, presented cheetahs to the Great Khan or Emperor of China in the early fourteenth century. (The Golden Horde was the name given to the western part of the Mongol empire of Genghis Khan, and consisted of a mix of Turks and Mongols who made up the aristocracy. Their territory covered China, Mongolia, Russia, Tibet down to the Indus River, and all the way west beyond Baghdad to the Euphrates River – an enormous and powerful empire which flourished from the mid-thirteenth to the end of the fourteenth century.) Since Ozbek also sent raptors to the Egyptian Mamelukes for the hunt, perhaps cheetahs came back in exchange. Certainly by the early fourteenth century Muslim merchants were conducting an active trade in cheetahs and other animals, which they brought via the Indian Ocean routes to the Yuan court; and cheetahs are known to have been in great demand and plentiful supply in Mongolian China. There were countless representations in the Mongolian Empire of hunting cats, especially in the form of glazed pottery tomb figurines portraying both cheetahs and caracals sitting behind a man on horseback.

In the West, the interest in using cheetahs for hunting began in Spain. There exists a piece of textile from the mid-eleventh century, probably showing a caracal rather than a cheetah, chained and riding pillion behind a hunter. Hunting with cheetahs, especially sitting behind the hunter on horseback, did not become popular until the thirteenth century, during the reign of the Holy Roman Emperor Frederick II (1220–50), who was based in Sicily. There and in southern Italy he kept hunting cheetahs and lynxes, thought to have been gifts from Muslim princes. Other cats were brought from North Africa through his agents in Malta and were probably the source of the three cheetahs the Emperor sent to England's Henry III as a princely gift. During Frederick's reign there was a marked flow of Muslim influence into Europe: in the Emperor's famed menagerie, the majority of handlers were Muslim and Frederick spoke to them in Arabic. We know that the man responsible for selecting, training and transporting the imperial cheetahs and lynxes and directing their handlers was a certain Rainaldin of Palermo, the Emperor's designated Chief Keeper. Also in the thirteenth century, when King Edward I of England sent the Persian ruler a number of hunting birds – the prized gyrfalcons – the Mongols sent him a cheetah in return.

The late fourteenth-century sketchbook of the Italian artist Giovannino de Grassi shows a tethered cheetah in the middle of a hunting scene. Pisanello's drawing of a cheetah (in the Louvre) from the first half of the fifteenth century is clearly the work of someone who could study the animal in detail from life. By the fifteenth and sixteenth centuries, the French monarchs had taken up hunting with imported cheetahs riding pillion behind them on their saddles, as they did elsewhere in Eurasia. But while this was considered exotic and elegant, it did not become 'mainstream', and its popularity in Europe was short-lived.

Oddly, hunting with cats reached its zenith in China at this same time, when both cheetahs and caracals arrived in Beijing as princely gifts from the rulers of Persia and Turkestan. And yet, in the early sixteenth century, Muslim traders travelling overland to China were still bringing cheetahs and caracals with them – they were highly valued and could be traded for precious cloth. How these animals travelled is a mystery, since traders mostly used camels to transport their merchandise and the temperature in the desert was around +40 degrees Celsius by day and, crossing over the mountain ranges, as low as −40 degrees at night.

The early sixteenth-century Chinese Emperor Zhengde established, in the royal palace in Beijing, a special area devoted to the hunting cats called (erroneously) the Leopard Quarter. Here the cheetahs were kept and trained to the chase. It remained in position until the end of the Ming dynasty in the mid-seventeenth century. Although the sport then died out in China, enthusiasm for it continued for several more centuries in India and Persia – perhaps thanks to a more ready supply of animals – but declined elsewhere, since cheetahs did not breed in captivity and suitable animals had to be imported.

Then there was the difficulty of finding trainers for the cheetahs, just as for the falcons and dogs coming from Europe and used in hunting. These skilled people had to be imported and encouraged to remain, as well as to train other staff to be as skilled as they were.

Hunting was not only a pleasure for the privileged – its accoutrements were also used as a diplomatic tool. The princely exchange of gifts connected to the chase led to an international traffic in animals and their keepers, and with this came an exchange of information about hunting practices. Foreign guests and diplomats talked endlessly about hunting, as well as taking part in the royal hunts. It was a cross-cultural bridge and, because it was assumed to be the consuming interest of all travellers, a socially safe topic. Hunting was such a passion among the elite that it was thought foreign courts were a vital source of information on the sport and that this should be tapped. Also, foreign animal handlers were to be nurtured and their skills cultivated, whether to do with 'hunting cats', birds or dogs.

It is thanks to the Mughals that we know so much about hunting with cheetahs, as they kept detailed records of everything to do with their hunting practices. Since Persian was the language of the Mughal court, the Persian term *yuz* or the Hindi *chita* was used for the cats. Royal hunts were very carefully staged affairs – nothing was left to chance. Game animals were even held in certain areas until the royal party arrived and only then released. This can be seen in a number of miniatures with animals herded into large enclosures before the hunters and cheetahs arrived for the killing spree. *See* colour plates for an illustration of a Mughal hunt.

Catching or trapping cheetahs seems not to have been difficult, despite their speed. Traps and nets were used mostly around their favourite 'scratching' or 'scent-marking' trees, the latter being the trees they sprayed with their urine to advertise their presence to other cheetahs.

The ideal cheetah for hunting was an adult female. Young cheetahs were rarely captured for training: animals that had already proved themselves for at least one or two seasons were preferred, and females more so than males since they were particularly skilled in hunting alone to feed themselves and their cubs. When females were captured with young, the cubs were abandoned to survive, or not, in the wild, while their mothers were taken away for taming, training and eventually put to work coursing.

The time spent on taming and training a cheetah to partake in a man-organised hunt would be anything between three months and a year depending on the kindness or otherwise of the trainer. The first stage consisted of tying up the captured cat, blindfolding it, depriving it of sleep and starving it into submission. Then it had to be made comfortable with human company, perhaps by being tethered on a busy street or walked on a leash. In India a cheetah would be taken to a village where women and children were paid to talk gently to it for hours.

The next step was for the cheetah to learn to ride a horse, sitting behind the rider on a pillion, a small platform attached to the back of the saddle. Tethered to the rider, the cheetah was encouraged to jump up on to the pillion of a small wooden horse with a treat left on it, so that it associated the pillion with food. Slowly the height of this wooden horse and its pillion was increased to that of a real horse. Once the cheetah was happy to jump to the required height, it had to become accustomed to sitting on a real horse with its handler – another delicate procedure.

Then the cheetah's hunting instincts must be renewed. This was done by the handler who had fed the cheetah since its capture, and who would kill an animal in front of the cat, allowing it to lap up its blood.

Next, the cheetah was taken into the field, wearing a hood as a falcon does to keep it calm and prevent it from becoming distracted. The handlers would separate an individual antelope from a herd, drive it to exhaustion, then unhood the cheetah and let it loose. The cheetah would easily capture the exhausted animal and hold in a choking grip until its handler came and despatched it.

The final trial was allowing the cheetah to choose its own prey target, to stalk, chase, capture and kill it. When this was done the cheetah was deemed ready to take part in a real royal hunt. Despite their intelligence, by no means all cheetahs came through their training programme successfully.

The same procedure was followed during a real hunt. If the cheetah was not needed to hunt again that day, a haunch would be cut off and given to it as its prize. If it was to hunt again, the blood was thought enough. All the cheetah had to do was to stalk, catch and then give up its kill to the handler. This was considered such thrilling sport that Indian princes would exchange one hunting ground for another at great expense.

When one of their cheetah charges failed to make a kill in a chase, Mughal trainers would feel the need to console them, assuring them they would do better next time. What appeared to be 'sulking' was really the cheetah resting to reduce its body temperature so it could run and hunt again. For hunting with a cheetah to be successful there had to be a great bond between the animal and its handler, just as there was and is between a hunting dog and its master.

The first of the six great Mughal emperors in India was a Central Asian Turk called Babur, born in 1483. He was a direct descendant of Genghis Khan through his mother, and through his father of Tamerlaine, the conqueror of Central Asia, who died in 1405. It was in his honour that the Mughals called themselves Timurids, as being 'of the House of Timur', or Tamerlaine.

When they came to India via Persia, the Mughals brought with them the cultural heritage of Uzbekistan, the artistic style influenced by the architecture of Samarkand, and by the beauty and gardens of Persia. They also brought with them trained cheetahs.

In the early sixteenth century most of the five hundred or so Indian maharajahs had menageries which contained cheetahs caught either in Asia or in Africa and often presented as royal gifts. Over time, some of these inevitably escaped, becoming feral, which later gave rise to the belief that cheetahs were native to India. One of the proofs that there were no indigenous cheetahs in India is that the terrain and environment were unsuitable. The uneven ground of the grasslands made running fast difficult, and the presence of large packs of wolves, as well as hyenas, tigers and leopards, would have made it impossible for the lighter cat to survive in the wild.

Since the Mughal Empire lasted from the mid-sixteenth until the mid-nineteenth century, during that time many European travellers took part in or observed the royal cheetah hunt and sent descriptions home. Father Monserrate, a priest who spent two years at the court of Babur's grandson Akbar in the 1580s, wrote that he never encountered nor heard of the existence of wild cheetahs, but did see Akbar hunting with his tame ones. He recorded how 'the panthers are drawn by horses, under the care of keepers, to the place where game is feeding'. Several of them, blindfolded, were seated on the cart which, oddly, was often pulled by blackbuck, the cheetahs' favourite prey, with the cats attached to the sides of the cart and kept hungry. When the cheetah was brought near the game – either blackbuck or chinkara (Asian gazelle) – the blindfold was removed, it jumped down from the cart and was released to stalk and then dash after its quarry.

With the cheetah in full pursuit of the game, the hunters would chase after it on horseback. When they reached the cheetah holding a buck by the neck, they would dismount and slit the throat of the struggling, captured animal. Blackbuck were so used to seeing the local carts bringing a cheetah near their herds, it is not surprising that they did not suspect danger. Nevertheless, the cheetah did not always catch its prey and had not more than a fifty percent chance of success.

As well as riding pillion on the back of horses, cheetahs were also launched from the backs of elephants and camels, or from a cart called a *hackerie*, or led to the antelopes on foot in the open, or from an ambush.

There are many depictions of elegantly dressed Mughals on horseback following cheetahs pursuing antelope or wild boar, giving the impression the hunters were in competition with wild cheetahs for the antelopes – but in fact, the big cats were tame and the hunters followed only to finish off the prey caught in the cheetah's choking hold.

The Mughals saw to it that their prize cheetahs had their own tents in the royal encampment and were sometimes carried on a litter with a canopy for shade. Each of the Emperor Akbar's cheetahs had decorated collars with leashes and brocaded saddle cloths. A truly favoured animal received a bejewelled collar with precious stones, and a beating drum would precede it when it was taken out to hunt as a sign of the elevation it had attained.

Favourite cheetahs were also given names and even titles following a great feat. One such was a cheetah belonging to Akbar, which came with him when the Emperor's army was encamped in Jaipur in 1572. The contemporary record states that the Emperor was devoted to hunting with his *citas* and after assigning cheetahs to other guests, he went off himself with some special attendants. One of these let loose a royal cheetah called Citr Najan at an antelope.

'Suddenly there appeared in front of them a stream which was twenty-five yards broad. The deer leapt into the air to the height of a spear and a half and conveyed itself across. The *cita* in its eagerness took the same course, cleared the stream and seized the deer. On beholding this astounding occurrence the spectators raised a cry of amazement and there was great rejoicing and astonishment. The Khedive raised the rank of that *cita* and made him chief of the *citas*. He also ordained that as a special honour, and as a pleasure to men, a drum should be beaten in front of that *cita*.'

This leap was considered so amazing (even if the width of the stream was exaggerated) that the event was recorded in a painting in the *Akbarnama* – the official chronicle of Akbar's reign, preserved in the Victoria and Albert Museum in London. It shows Citr Najan on the neck of a fallen male blackbuck across the stream while Akbar, astride a chestnut horse, appears to be calming his mount with his right hand while reining him in with his left to prevent him attempting the jump and at the same time looking at the cheetah across the stream. Citr Najan's empty bullock cart is nearby, with an attendant holding a rope. In the background there is another attendant on horseback with a cheetah sitting on its back. Eight female and two subadult male blackbuck are seen running away.

Akbar's rules for caring for his best cheetahs stated they were to be provided with five pounds (about two and a quarter kilograms) of fresh meat a day. It is hard to believe he kept herds of hundreds of thousands of antelope and wild boar, as he would have needed to do in order to feed so many cheetahs.

Hundreds, if not thousands of cheetahs were paraded at the end of a leash or in carts all over the Mughal Empire, yet were rarely seen in the wild. But with such numbers of kept animals, naturally there were escapees, and Akbar employed special bands of 'cheetah catchers' to try to find and retrieve them. They were often caught after falling into pits, and it is written that Akbar would 'immediately mount a swift horse and ride to the spot'. Since such places could have been anywhere in his vast empire, this too seems unlikely, but it is known he cared greatly for these, his favourite animals. When he could, he watched to see that they were lifted gently from the hole into which they had fallen and treated them like beloved friends. It was said that Akbar 'made hunting a means of gaining knowledge, and he loved gaining knowledge about the "citahs"'.

Despite the vast number of these cats he owned, it is recorded that during his lifetime Akbar had *only one litter* – born to a female which escaped and mated with a feral partner. Mother and cubs were treated better than honoured guests and all the cubs apparently survived to adulthood. There is almost no other record of a mother with cubs among trained and tame cheetahs in India, and yet to supply the thousands of cheetahs taken for centuries to adorn the courts of emperors, kings and noblemen in Europe and the East, the cats can have had no problem breeding in the wild.

Stress is a known deterrent to cheetah breeding, as is being overweight which they might well be when kept as spoiled pets. Sometimes when cheetahs did not breed they would be moved to try at other locations, which only stressed them more.

The tradition of hunting with cheetahs continued under Akbar's son Jahangir (1605–27), who is said to have hunted as often on horseback with a cheetah riding pillion behind him as he did with elephants drawing his carriage and his assistants holding raptors. Like his father, Jahangir seems to have been particularly sensitive to his cheetahs' moods and to have taken great trouble to bond with his favourites which, from all accounts, behaved like friendly dogs with their handlers. When King James I of England, a contemporary of Jahangir, sent his ambassador, Sir Thomas Roe, to India, he reported back that the maharajahs' cheetahs formed part of their ceremonial processions, seated grandly in their wheeled carts with their keepers, and that these stately animals impressed him greatly.

Many artists were drawn to such ceremonial events, and details of exotic hunts can be seen emblazoned on metalware, textiles and figurines, as well as in pictures, all circulating throughout India, China, Korea, Japan and the West. However, there is only one painting from the Mughal period of a cheetah mother with cubs – and she is accompanied by a male, something which never happened since females raise their cubs alone, so this picture cannot have been drawn from life.

Sultan Tipoo, the famous 18th-century Indian ruler of Mysore who defied the English during their attacks on French-held territory in India, was another cheetah enthusiast. Known as the Tiger of Mysore, he kept cheetahs which he fed by hand and they were said to jump around him like pet dogs. As well as deer, their favourite prey, Tipoo's cheetahs hunted hares, foxes and jackals. It was thought that he imported his cats from Madras, an important centre for trade, but it is not certain whether these were brought from Africa; it is also possible that they came with the Mughals from Central Asia or Persia.

When Tipoo was finally defeated, his goods were distributed among members of the British East India Company. Among the victors' spoils were three 'Chetas or Hunting Tygers, with a hunting cart, two trained bullocks and every other article for hunting the Cheta in England in the same manner as the royal hunt of the Sultan was conducted'. The elaborate clothing the Sultan wore also came with the animals to England and was presented to King George III, but the king never hunted with the cheetahs.

These were not the first 'hunting cats' to be presented to the British royal family. Forty years earlier, a cheetah from the British Commander-in-Chief in Madras had been given to the Duke of Cumberland, son of George II, for the royal menagerie at Windsor. An attempt to course with it in the Great Park failed, since so many people had come to watch that the cheetah refused to move. However, the artist George Stubbs recorded the incident in a painting (*see* colour plates). He shows the cheetah's two Indian handlers exhorting it to chase the stag, which is seen observing them from a distance.

Reports of wild cheetahs in India, in particular in Hyderabad State, maintaining that they attacked livestock in dense forest areas do not quite ring true. At the time, cheetahs had not yet acclimatised themselves to forests – they much preferred to hunt in open spaces where they could use their speed. The ones in the forests were either escapees from a royal menagerie – their speed was mentioned by one witness, an old India hand – or they were leopards, since their distinctive black tear marks were not noted.

It is on record that old cheetahs were released when they were no longer of use to their master. There is a charming story that one such animal was found in the early twentieth century near Osmania University in Hyderabad, where the villagers fed it scraps. When the ruling Nizam heard, he had the animal caught, well housed and given as much as it could eat 'for having served and provided good sport and it was proper that Man should take care of him'.

In 1900 the famous French travel writer Pierre Loti described the cheetahs he had seen in Udaipur in Rajasthan: 'Servants lead tame cheetahs belonging to the king through the streets. They are led on slips so they may become accustomed to crowds. They wear little embroidered caps tied under their chins with a bow.'

Having read so much about hunting with cheetahs, I was eager to find out where so many of them had come from during the three centuries of Mughal rule. Some had obviously been brought from Central Asia when the Mughals conquered India in the sixteenth century, but since the beginning of the eighteenth century there can be little doubt that they came from Africa, and later they were even bred on farms in Kenya. Certainly by the nineteenth century – if not before – coursing was the fashion in British India, and cheetahs were sourced as a luxury for the rich – there are many references to their cost. During the nineteenth century, the official records state that some 200,000 wolves were killed in India, 150,000 leopards and some 80,000 tigers. In the same period only about forty cheetahs were seen or shot, but then of course they didn't occur naturally in the wild.

Before World War II, there was a famous hunter in Kenya called Raymond Hook – quite a character, it seems – who would capture cheetahs by chasing them on horseback until they were run to exhaustion. Then, surrounded by dogs and unable to escape, they would be muzzled and tied to a tree for some time to starve them and break their spirit before being brought back to his establishment. Despite the apparent cruelty of this method, Hook was known to have great love and respect for cheetahs and it seems he handled them well and knew a great deal about them and their dispositions. It could take up to six months for him to train them to trust their captors completely, and he was then able to sell them to a maharajah. The training involved the cheetah being blindfolded and the trainer approaching it with food so that it would associate him with feeding. A collar and then a lead were put on and the cheetah was taught, still blindfolded, to go for walks like a dog. Next it learned to chase meat attached to a rope – as Tess had done with me. Slowly the trainer increased the distances and, when that succeeded, the cheetah was considered ready to hunt antelope. When it saw the buck, it was released to chase it. If it failed to capture the prey after a fast dash, it would sit down to catch its breath, wait for its cart, be given food and taken home.

An interesting point that Hook discovered was that in ancient times, cheetahs 'appeared frequently on monuments whenever a civilisation reached some sort of peak. As soon as the civilisation declined it swiftly disappeared'. The year the last three cheetahs were killed in India also marked the end of the British Raj.

ABOVE An Ancient Egyptian fresco depicts a hunting party out with a cheetah.

ABOVE LEFT A cheetah offered as tribute to an Egyptian king, *c.* 1700 BC.

ABOVE RIGHT Tame cheetahs drawn by the Italian artist Giovannino de' Grassi in the 14th century.

ABOVE A blindfolded and tamed cheetah waits patiently until it is time to hunt. Favoured Mughal cheetahs were dressed royally with cloaks and jewels.

ABOVE *Cheetah and Stag with Two Indians*, George Stubbs (1724–1806). This painting was apparently inspired by an incident when a hunting cheetah was brought from India to Windsor and pitched against a stag *see* p.158.

ABOVE A Mughal hunt showing three hunting cheetahs and one yet to be released, *see* p.155.

ABOVE *The Cavalcade of the Magi* fresco by Benozzo Gozzoli from the walls of the Medici's tiny chapel in Florence. The animal riding pillion behind the page in blue was described as a 'spotted leopard' but is clearly a cheetah, as can be seen from its tear markings, as is the one on the ground.

Hook's training methods were so successful that others took note and it was he who proved what the Mughals had practised – that cheetah cubs could not be trained to hunt. Cheetahs had to be caught fully grown, when they were already successful hunters. With speed being the cheetah's greatest asset, Hook noticed that the longer the animal remained in captivity, the more its bursts of lightning speed would slow down. Once Hook's animals were successfully trained, they were sold to an Indian trader in Nanyuki, Kenya, who mothered them, calling them 'his beautiful children' and carefully shipped them to Bombay to be forwarded on to the Indian princes. This practice continued until the 1950s.

Some Indians not only purchased their cheetahs from Africa but also travelled there to hunt with them. This was done in great style. Vehicles shipped from England and the USA included a mobile wireless receiving and transmitting station, a van for cinematography, an armoured car, well-equipped kitchens, generating plants, lorries, a medical van with an x-ray unit, and a caravan hauled on an articulated trailer powered by a Scammell engine. Also there were several Elsan chemical lavatories and gaily striped canvas booths to put them in...

A motorcycle rider would be sent back to the base convoy with full details of the day's bag to appear as a news item in the maharajah's state the following day: 'Today, His Highness shot etc.' That maharajah's return home was as elaborately staged as his arrival and safari in Africa: he would travel to the ship the day before she sailed in a Rolls-Royce already 'furnished in lion skin rugs and upholstery selected from the pelts he had shot himself'. Lions, which were also imported into India, mostly from Africa, bred quite well in captivity. But they were easier to hunt in Africa and a lion skin was a vital sign of the maharajah's prestige.

These rich hunters paid well not only to kill big game but also to capture cheetahs to take back with them to be trained for coursing. The writer Alastair Scobie noted that there were big farms throughout Africa kept by hunters and game catchers specifically to service international demand, not only for big game but also for the maharajahs' menageries. Sometimes these animals were hunted but, he observed, never the cheetah – they were the 'hunters' dogs'.

Not until 1972, when Prime Minister Indira Gandhi abolished the Indian princes' privileges, did African wildlife cease to be exported to India. Sadly, this did not increase the dwindling numbers of game in Africa since Europeans came in their droves to hunt the 'big four' – elephant, rhino, buffalo and lion – all now either endangered or vulnerable. As for the cheetah, the weakest of the big cats, its territory shrinks every year, as do the antelope herds it needs to sustain it.

Most of my researches into hunting with cheetahs had taken me back several centuries and to exotic places such as China and India. But I also came across a bizarre story from a rather less glamorous place – Essex.

There was a brief period during the 1930s when cheetahs were brought to England to be raced at Romford Stadium – a popular but short-lived sport among the aristocracy. It seems greyhound racing was losing its draw and someone had the bright idea of adding a little excitement by having the dogs race against cheetahs! Although at first there was some concern that the cheetahs might eat the dogs, soon it was seen they had been trained to chase the meat on the 'rabbit'.

From the first race it was abundantly clear that things would not work out. The cheetah was so much faster than the greyhound, it was not a race. Then, when several cheetahs were put to race against one another, that did not work either. The 'rabbit' lure held little attraction for them unless a large piece of meat was attached, but this was quickly caught and eaten, whereupon the winner sat down. Cheetahs were simply too intelligent to be persuaded to run after the 'rabbit' like greyhounds. Not only did they cut corners and run across the stadium to get to the meat, but once it was eaten, they would lose interest, sit down or even lie down and sleep. Competition was not in their repertoire and after the first season, the twelve trained cheetahs employed did not race again. However, as a publicity stunt it had worked and people came back to Romford Stadium.

CHAPTER VII

While learning learn about the lives of cheetahs, I continued with my efforts to train Tess and delighted in her company. Now true to her full name, Vitesse, she ran after the meat tied to the string behind the pick-up truck so well that I really had to put my foot down on the accelerator and drive dangerously fast on our bumpy driveway through the 'home jungle' to prevent her catching the prize too soon.

What a thrill it was to see her in her young prime. After her daily training run with either me or one of the 'Tess Team' driving, she would join me on the terrace, facing far-distant Beira, and I would read to her what I was learning about cheetahs in past centuries. Ever polite, when I paused she would often nudge me with her paw, since I may have stopped my rhythmic brushing. Both Papi and Rosemarie thought I was absurd, but I really had no one else to talk to and she always listened – which they did not!

Tess and I – we were a unit in my living quarters – still had surprises. One morning Papi could not start the Land Rover and I heard him turning the key again and again – an annoying sound not far from my windows, accompanied by ascending invective. Tess was sitting up – dawn was her best time – and then a shout, followed by others, had us running to the front door. The routine at the end of the day was that Papi's vehicle would be taken away to be washed, filled with petrol at our own pump and generally seen to before being driven back to the front of the house to stay there overnight, ready for his departure early the next day. But on this particular morning, several of the house staff armed with sticks and a furious Papi were gathered around the open bonnet of the vehicle, not too close either. It seemed that not long after it had been brought back, and when the engine was still warm, a large snake – they were all referred to as 'mamba' and usually were – had slithered under the bonnet and settled over the interior rather like a duvet, preventing the motor from starting. When Schultz opened the bonnet to see what was wrong, there it lay, draped like a heavy rug, smothering the fan belt and everything else. I told Tess this was 'men's work' and we crept back indoors.

These were happy months with Tess. She had grown into a fine big cheetah, very light boned, although she ate a lot (said Eduardo), and she was most affectionate to me, Papi, Rosemarie and the house staff. Outsiders she viewed with suspicion and, if they came up to her, she would invariably try to trip them up as they walked. Because she was so friendly with us, visitors would never anticipate or understand her distrust of them. (Clever girl – I always worried she would approach strangers when she went back into the bush and perhaps be caught or shot.) We went for long walks together, Tess always wearing her halter and lead – I dreaded her running off and hunting when I had only Francisco with me and the hunters had other things to do. We had taken enough of their working days for her education.

It was at this time that Antonio emerged from his kitchen Hades and asked to speak to Rosemarie once again. His brother had given him a gift for her, my father and me. Very seriously, he presented us with three small, spongy bags hanging from a leather thong, which he wanted us to wear at all times about our necks. It did not look very attractive and we instinctively recoiled. But Antonio claimed that his brother was anxious and insisted the 'juju' amulet would keep us 'safe'. Moreover, he urged us to bury a number of other little spongy bags he gave us around the property. Witch doctor 'med'cin' is never cheap and Papi, born a sceptic and one still, despite his near-death experience due to one witch doctor and rescue at the hands of another, felt this was too expensive and too much trouble. But Antonio was adamant and, with tears in his eyes, repeated again and again that we were in danger. Had another spell been cast on us all, perhaps? He looked distraught and said he had no idea.

Finally, Rosemarie and I felt we had to calm and reassure him, saying we would do it even if Ba'as would not help us. Over the following week, feeling like idiots and accompanied by Francisco and a couple of workers (plus Tess and Daisy), we drove around our perimeter fence planting the little 'juju' bags – and did not mention them again in front of Papi.

We forgot about it until a month or so later when we were told by one of our foremen during our regular evening clinic that he had heard a plague of red locusts was coming in our direction, blown by strong winds from Tanzania. If true, this was very dangerous. These creatures eat at an incredible rate and target food crops, especially our two biggest – citrus and maize. To find out if there was anything to this story, Papi arranged for us to go up again in the dreaded Piper Comanche.

We circled the farm on a glorious sunny day in a cloudless, blue sky, zooming down to inspect the neat lines of fruit trees and the maize fields, spotting antelope at the river's edge and waving back at the village children waving up at us. I had almost forgotten why we were up there when Papi pointed to a low dark cloud in the far distance. 'That,' he said, 'is a locust swarm. Fortunately it does not look very large, but perhaps it has more behind it – I cannot see.' We flew further, to the farm of neighbours, but saw no one about below. 'They are often away on safari,' Papi told me, since they did not farm, just enjoyed living in this beautiful countryside. We were brought back to Maforga, landed and quickly gathered the domestic staff together. Papi said just three words: 'Red locusts coming' – which sent them running in every direction while he drove off to tell the workers and send word to Chief Aboiye, who would relay the bad news to the other villages.

Everyone knew their role – it had happened before. Humans and animals had to be confined indoors with at least three days' supply of food and water. Chimney flues had to be blocked up from inside; windows shuttered; all pipes blocked – catching water from gutters and passing into the house; the boiler exit, the kitchen chimney, all closed off. Air vents checked to ensure they were covered with close wire netting. No locust must be allowed to enter buildings – 'But they will,' said Papi ominously.

Twenty-four hours after our aerial view of the distant dark cloud, we received word that the swarm was only eight kilometres away. Any staff or workers with families living nearby were sent home to prepare for the onslaught. From the end of the day we remained inside, the dogs whingeing and a confused Tess dribbling me a football, hoping to be allowed to go out to play.

To kill time, Papi, Rosemarie and I played three-handed bridge (not my favourite game without a fourth) or two of us played canasta. We played Scrabble in German and English (which made cheating easier), even Monopoly, which Papi hated. Another day, and then another, and although a few locusts did get into the house, we peeped out between the shuttered windows and could see no great dirty red cloud of them, nor did we hear the tell-tale screeching noise I had been told to expect, nor their collision with the shuttered windows, which would sound like hailstones. Peeping out, we saw some had landed on the terrace, but not many, and other clever ones found a way inside the house – to the delight of Tess, who would jump up to catch them and then eat them with a crunch, crunch, spitting out the wings.

On the fourth day, Eduardo drove up to the front door and was let in. 'I came down your jungle drive – nothing has been eaten – they have not come your way and have passed on. It's amazing – all the farms on the way here are stripped bare. The wind must have lifted them up from your valley.'

We exclaimed in delight and thanked God for the blessed wind! The maize crops and the citrus were both safe and we looked like having an excellent harvest that year. Papi always said that the produce of one good year covered the losses of several bad. There were downsides to the rich soil and good rainfall – insects and countless diseases to affect the different harvests – but today the mood at Maforga was buoyant.

Our workers came back – none of their small planted plots on our land had been destroyed. How fortunate we had been! Only Papi had 'that look' that I came to associate with his innate scepticism. Quietly he drew me aside and said, 'Let's go up and take a look.' By that he meant borrowing the Piper and pilot again – and so we did.

What we saw was incredible, astonishing. We flew in every direction from the farm – north, south, east and west – and always the same view: our land, both cultivated and the large jungle area beyond, was lush and green. All around our border, the foliage and crops had been eaten clean by the locusts on their way to the coast where, I was informed, they would head out to sea, find no more land and drown – to the joy of predator fish. Of all the vegetation in the swarm's path to the coast, only ours was completely unaffected – totally green – crops and trees untouched. Had they missed us for some reason? The wind had been suggested, the lay of the land, the curve of the great valley... And would they be coming back?

Returning to the house, we told Rosemarie, who was busy with the dogs – they were behaving strangely, as if spooked by something, two of them trying to crawl under beds. 'Perhaps a lion or a leopard, driven close to the house by the locusts?' she ventured and ordered tea, which came in with an ashen-faced Antonio. His expression was enough to make Rosemarie look at him quizzically. 'Antonio, I want you to tell me honestly. You knew something?' Blank. 'About the locusts, coming, didn't you?' He looked at his feet. 'Was it the juju? What was in those amulets your brother gave us to plant around the farm?' He shook his head and said he did not know. 'They saved us from the red locusts, didn't they?' He looked dazed and rather baffled himself, but nodded. Rosemarie patted his shoulder. 'You can be sure I will reward you both.' And as he left, patently relieved, she remained sitting with a strange expression, deep in her own thoughts.

Tess was not bothered by any of it and lay sleeping, but I saw Papi and Rosemarie exchanging looks, although they said no more. Later I asked Rosemarie if it was really possible that the nasty little charms we had planted could have kept the locusts away. It seemed so absurd. She just looked at me for a while and then said she honestly did not know, but we would go to church on Sunday as usual, thank God and talk to the priest. Papi remained dubious even after all he had seen of African magic, black or white. No one could explain it except by saying perhaps it was the lay of our land. Rosemarie, a believing Catholic – Papi also, but more cynical – simply said, 'God works in mysterious ways.' I will probably never know, but I did not stop wearing the leather thong with the amulet that the cook's brother had given me for as long as I was with them in Africa.

Tess continued to provide us with entertainment. One day Chief Aboiye came to Papi to ask for his help in starting up a small beekeeping enterprise in his village. Papi immediately handed him over to Rosemarie, saying he was not comfortable around bees! Since Tess and I were in the vicinity, Rosemarie had me come to listen to what the chief had to say.

He told us he had found a wild hive and wanted to bring it to the village and enlarge it. Did he know anything about beekeeping? Oh yes, he claimed, he did, but he would need a little capital and then to be supplied with jars and lids, and could he put the name of the farm on a label and sell the honey in the local store in Gondola?

Rosemarie rightly said she would have to see and taste the honey first and then decide. A little while later, we had quite forgotten about the chief – who had eyed Tess in a way that I did not like at all, no doubt thinking what her coat would fetch him – when we heard he had come to the office and would like to speak with Rosemarie again.

Curious, and taking Tess with me, I went with Rosemarie down to the office near the garages. The chief looked smarter than usual, his cloak of antelope hide attached on one shoulder with a shell of some kind and the leather quite stiff and sticking out on one side. Underneath, I could see he was wearing a pair of khaki shorts and nothing else. Around his neck a necklace of some other small shells and, as always, in his right hand his staff of office with a spear head ringed with red feathers.

He bowed to Rosemarie and then to me and winked (!) and smiled at Tess, who growled back. Clever girl. Then he brought out from somewhere under the amazing stiff cloak a small glass jar, the kind that jam comes in, with a lid, and what looked like honey inside, a slightly smoky-grey golden colour.

'Memsahib, here is honey,' he said proudly and offered the jar.

Rosemarie graciously took it and we walked home and ordered tea with toast. We had to try the honey! And we did with delight: it was totally delicious. We put it in the tea as well – excellent. Not grainy at all, it ran smoothly from the end of a spoon. I offered Tess some on a plate and she lapped it up, although I was not sure how good it was for a cheetah's digestion.

And so Rosemarie became Chief Aboiye's partner and advanced the money he asked for. Sadly the honey production was rather sporadic, but when it came we bought all of it, used it in the house and gave some as gifts to friends – we dared not sell it without knowing what was in it and there really was not enough to make it a commercial proposition.

One day when Tess was eighteen months old and we were walking around the orange orchard, Francisco mentioned that there was a honey harvest in progress at Chief Aboiye's village, would I like to see? The inhabitants of some other villages on the farm would be there as well. The chief's honey was much in demand and also used on wounds, which Francisco assured me it healed.

So I went to the village with Tess, Francisco and both Rodrigo and Assia – neither would let Tess go without them. It was probably a little unkind of me to take Tess, who was bound to frighten everyone at first, but she was wearing her halter and had Assia holding her lead. I wanted them to see what a fine animal she was. Perhaps then they would realise what they had done to her mother by setting the trap that caused her death. Ravo had told me that the trap had been for antelope and that the cheetah should not have been caught, but that did not make their fault any the less in my eyes.

Chief Aboiye led us to the end of the village, past fifteen or so small huts. Only one, his own, had a boma, a fence about my height made of wooden staves so I could not see what was inside: from the noise I judged it contained the chief's pigs. Tess was quite excited by their smell – very pungent – but Assia had had the foresight to feed her before we set out. At the back of the village I saw some ten or more open wooden boxes, measuring about forty-five by forty centimetres, laid out on trestle tables. Into these were hung, vertically and lengthwise, wooden-topped slides hinged to the edges of the boxes.

I could hear buzzing but saw no bees flying around; then the chief indicated that one of his people should lift out a wooden-edged tray. The inside was made of honeycomb and looked full of honey. The man quickly slipped the tray back when he saw Tess coming forward. Francisco translated for me that the village was making good money from the sale of their honey and they were very pleased with our investment. I asked if we had been repaid and I was assured we had credit for at least a year's supply of honey!

That being the case, I asked for some honey to be poured on to a plate for us to try with our fingertips and out came a saucepan full. It was poured on to a metal tray – none too clean, I thought, as I carefully dipped my finger into the top of the runny honey without touching the base. It had the same delicious smoky-dark flavour as the sample we had tried up at the farm. As I was savouring my finger and before I realised what was happening, Tess had pushed past Assia and stuck her black nose into the tray, pulled it out and was busily licking it clean! It was definitely time to go – I had visions of a cheetah honey-hive thief in Gorongosa National Park. What if the locals in the villages in the park made honey and she had developed a taste for it? Our honey-eating cheetah would not last long.

As Tess neared maturity, we talked more and more about releasing her. I knew both Papi and Rosemarie worried that I had become too attached to her. *But so had they*. The character of a home-reared cheetah is totally affectionate, gentle, adorable, funny – how could anyone not love her? She had begun to copy the dogs and to raise her paw on to my knee when sitting by me as if to ask for something, and with a plaintive look in her clear amber eyes... *was it freedom she wanted?*

Eduardo came to see Papi privately, and then together with Rosemarie they came to me. It was an awkward moment and I knew something was coming. Papi looked at Rosemarie, hoping she would speak, but she shook her head as if to say it was his role. Papi drew himself up: 'My darling girl (always a bad start), I know we have discussed when and where we will let Tess go so that she has the security of living in Gorongosa National Park, but I have been anxious that she is too tame for her own good. If she meets humans she may well come up to them and want some comforting. Where I think she should be released is at least a bit off the main tourist routes although, as you know, cheetahs cover a lot of ground. I do not think she will look for you in the park, only at the place where she was released, if that (clearing of throat). What we want to prepare you for is that... *Tess might not make it in the wild.*'

We were outside on the terrace leaning on the balcony and looking towards the distant coast. I must have turned pale because

Papi had me sit down on one of the sofas backing the wall, and then they all sat.

'It will be hard for her to succeed immediately hunting for herself. You and I and all of us have discussed this, although we know she can do it and have seen her. Eduardo and I think we should take her to the area where we plan to release her, sometime before we do. Just day trips so that she associates the place with food and friendship. We'll take a leg of game for her, so that should any of us want to reassure ourselves that she is well, we can do it from there, and then that is the place she will know to come to.

'I must be brutal with you, my darling. Eduardo, who knows about cheetahs,' and here he took my hand, 'wants you to be prepared for the fact that she might not survive having to feed herself, and that if she does, that she will most probably *not* come back or even hear your taped calls. I am sorry to have to tell you this, but Rosemarie, Eduardo and I felt we should prepare you.' And they exchanged looks.

I remember feeling sick to my stomach, as if it had turned inside out – and there was Tess, lolling on the floor near us, half-asleep and not understanding what we were talking about.

Only much later did I realise that they hoped Tess would never be called back by me and my tape recordings. She was to be wild, but they had wanted to give me the illusion that I had not lost her completely...

Then Papi continued: 'Here is the problem. Giving her something to eat is the best way we have of ensuring that she knows the place where we might leave her food. But if we were caught with even a leg of game in the park, it would look as if we had been poaching –

ABOVE With HRH Prince Michael of Kent, sitting with Kapama cheetahs.
BELOW Showing the difference between a king and a regular cheetah's coats.

ABOVE With Lente Roode, releasing cheetahs from her Hoedspruit Endangered Species Centre at Kapama, South Africa.

Above and Below We watched as the cheetahs, wearing GPS collars for easy tracking, took stock of their new surroundings and eventually wandered off into the wild.

ABOVE With Laurie Marker at the Cheetah Conservation Fund in Namibia.
BELOW With Lente Roode at Kapama.

there are no hunting concessions there. So I would have to go with Rodrigo or Assia to our hunting concession, kill an antelope there, wrap up a leg and hide it in the car, and join Rosemarie, Eduardo, you, Tess and Francisco at a rendezvous point before crossing the river into the park. We would have to time it carefully: you cannot be kept waiting with Tess in the car – she gets too excited thinking we are going on safari. We would wait for you and cross in both vehicles – our cars are known, after all. Then we could picnic in the release spot with Tess eating her antelope leg and still attached with a long rein to her harness.

'I think we should do this once a week until the release date – Eduardo?' Eduardo nodded agreement.

I had lots of questions, but they could not be answered. What if she was injured – who would know? Who would help her? What if she wanted to come home… ? Oh, I was becoming idiotic!

Papi was ready to go on:

'Then when the day comes to release her, we will bring her to the park earlier, so that it is nearer her usual hunting time… but without her harness and without any meat, so she will be hungry. We will walk with her to where the dense bush starts – and wish her well. I think that hunger will make her move on in.' I had tears in my eyes and bent down to stroke Tess so that no one could see. Papi went on: 'Eduardo and Ravo both think she will be so curious and hungry that she will be quite bold and walk ahead, since she will be accustomed to the area. We should not stay too long, but just leave. Then we should continue to bring her part of a carcass, something that does not look poached, say once a week, in case she has not yet established her own home range and is starving.'

Rosemarie was sitting next to me with her arm around me and the tears ran down my face. Papi continued: 'Nor can we do much calling with your tape either. I think we have to get her used to a whistle from today. Whistle should mean food. Just in case its sound travels further – that's why I don't like you using your voice.'

I knew he was right, but we did not have much time. Tess was to be released in mid to late September, six weeks or so before she would be two years old; she might well be coming into oestrus by then, and it was important (Eduardo said) that she be released before that happened. It would be the rainy season, but we had to hope for the best – her leaving home before coming into oestrus was more important. Also, I was due to leave the farm and spend some time away, so we would time her release for immediately before my departure. But it was already July, which left us with not much more than two months in which to prepare her.

Papi had discussed the various options with Rosemarie, Eduardo and Ravo before telling me, so he was ready to put them into action. The next morning at dawn, he would set off for our hunting concession with Ravo and Assia to shoot an antelope. They would cut off its leg, wrap it up and have Assia stay there to wrap and hide the rest of the beast for collection on the way home. If anyone came, and the rangers knew him as one of our staff, he was to say he was there to prepare the site for our arrival. Papi and Ravo would then drive the short distance to the bridge. If they were early, they would stay out of sight, keeping a lookout for us, and meet us at ten o'clock near the pontoon.

At this point I had had enough and I allowed Rosemarie to take me to my room. Tess automatically followed and was let out, then came quickly back in again. She never took long before bed.

I had tried hard and I believe succeeded in not making Tess dependent on me – but it was I who had become dependent on her! Nor did my nonchalance fool anyone at Maforga – everyone knew 'the day' was coming. My greatest fear was that Tess would come into oestrus before we were ready to release her. That she would meet up with a male cheetah on the farm somewhere for a day, and I would have to let her go off into the wild already pregnant. Would she have time to establish a home range before she gave birth? Would another male kill her or her cubs? Eduardo said no – but that her time was approaching. She had chosen and established a 'scratching tree' in the garden, standing on her hind legs and scratching it with her paws. Such trees are also called 'playing trees', places where cheetahs will congregate and leave their scent. By scratching at one particular tree trunk in the park, a rather nice acacia, was Tess inviting a male cheetah to visit her? I asked Eduardo and he looked down and pursed his lips. I could tell he did not like it: another reason for accepting that her departure time was creeping up on us. I must work on the whistle. She must learn to obey the whistle…

Although I was dreading the day when I had to send my beloved Tess to her new life in the wild, to survive with all its various challenges and without our protection, I had to admit, looking at her, that at almost twenty-four months she was fully mature. Despite not being allowed outside without her harness so we could catch her more easily if we needed to, in the late afternoons she was spending some time alone on the farm, which made me imagine she was already looking for a mate rather than a small buck. When she returned just before nightfall, she would always greet me with much purring, her head bumping my legs, or catching one of them with a quick swipe from a front paw in play ambush, and then licking my fingers – I had never allowed her to lick my face.

Before we settled down together on the floor of my room as usual, I decided to measure her. When I stood, so did she and allowed me to pass the tape all around her while she tried to catch it as I wrote. She stood almost seventy-five centimetres tall from her shoulder to the floor, a little less than an adult male but more than the average height of a leopard. Although female cheetahs are smaller than males, I felt she would still grow taller. I tried to get her to sit on my scales to be weighed but failed, and she was too big for me to hold in my arms, weigh us both and deduct my weight. I noticed that her whiskers were still short and rather inconspicuous – should they be longer? I must ask Eduardo. Her black tear streaks ran down as before, sharp black lines from the inner corners of her beautiful, inscrutable tawny eyes down the side of her nose to the outer corners of her mouth. I brushed her daily and gently on her underbelly which was white, as was the fluffy tip of her long, strong tail. To me, she seemed to be in prime condition. How could I say goodbye to this loving companion, my beautiful friend, Vitesse?

It was Eduardo who chose the date of her release, since he was watching her carefully for signs of oestrus: he thought it might be late since she had never (to our knowledge) met another cheetah, but he preferred to err on the side of caution. Naturally we accepted that he was right. More practice with the whistle – she was beginning to obey it. Oh please!

The next two weeks were among the happiest and the saddest of my young life. Tess and I played catch with Daisy and a much chewed football on the lawn and sometimes the other dogs would join in. Their rough and tumble with the cheetah was becoming rather strenuous and I called a halt before one of them was injured. There were seven dogs, one Tess and me, and even though Daisy played on our side, we were outnumbered.

Every week we repeated the trip across the pontoon up to the chosen 'picnic site'. We would produce the leg of antelope, talk and walk around for an hour or so, practise the whistle and then drive home. There, Tess and I continued to go for our daily walks together, followed by Francisco and now also either Rodrigo or Assia. They too looked less cheerful than usual. At this point, I carried only a lead and no longer bothered with the harness – somehow I knew she would not leave me until her official departure time came. She had always enjoyed jumping up to catch francolin, one of the few birds I had seen her eat, and I think they played with her to make her leap as high as possible. Several flew low over her to tempt her, but although she jumped merrily, she failed to catch one on our last walks.

Every morning of those precious days, she woke me at dawn, urging me with her little chirrup call to come out with her, and I did. Magical, unforgettable mornings. Everything around us took on an extra dimension, from the sunrise to the early-morning calls of the birds and Tess's imitations, and the calls of other wildlife, especially the laughing baboons. Although running free, she stayed near me as would a well-trained dog; and if she went ahead, she always looked back to make sure I was following. I hoped she would not do that when it was time for her to leave…

Three days before her release I saw her make a kill for the first time, a young oribi antelope that must have strayed from the others in its herd. We were walking not far from the dam and near the maize fields. Suddenly she flattened her body and I crouched down at once, as did Francisco and Assia behind me. We did not move; as yet I saw nothing, while Tess crept forward unbelievably slowly in about sixty-centimetres-high grass. At least five minutes passed before she launched herself forward, too fast for me to blink. I did not see the antelope until it was struggling with its neck in her jaws. None of us moved until she killed and released it. Then she began to open up the carcass and feed. As I approached to take a photograph, to my surprise she growled at me, so I backed off. Again I squatted, watched and waited. This was *her* breakfast, after all.

When she had eaten enough, Tess came to me purring, visibly pleased with herself, and then she let Assia lift her kill and carry it on his shoulders as we walked back home, her mouth and front paws quite bloodied. I was so proud. Assia and Rodrigo had told me of her prowess in hunting, but now I had seen for myself and felt somewhat more confident she could survive once she left us. I knew Gorongosa was teeming with small game; her prey would be animals half her own weight, and occasionally birds. Yes, Tess had learned enough to feed herself, but I was still anxious.

The day of her release was fast approaching, although I delayed every way I could. We had rehearsed it often. Papi and I would drive with her seated between us as she often was, but without her usual harness. If we saw anyone we would cover her with a blanket. We would drive across the Pungwe river on the pontoon bridge, follow the road running parallel to the edge of the park and stop at the campsite we'd chosen nearby. We had prepared a dry grass lean-to hide for her with her own old blanket from beside my bed should she wish to rest somewhere that smelt familiar in the early days. No one could associate us with it.

When the day came, it was bright and clear luckily, without rain. Although we knew that Tess had mastered the art of killing, still I worried. The drive went well, quicker this time than we expected. We didn't have to meet up with the other car, since we were not going to feed her. We crossed the pontoon, saw no one and Tess was getting fidgety, probably expecting her venison leg. We arrived at our spot and when Papi saw me fiddling and not opening my door, he gave me a swig from his hip flask – then I opened the door. Tess hopped out and hung about, waiting for the usual activity of making camp, which we were not going to do. She kept looking at me waiting for her supper. *Where's my leg of antelope?* I felt we should get on with it – drawn-out goodbyes with me in tears were not going to help.

Papi and I strode determinedly forwards across the grassy patch between our camping field and the beginning of the dense foliage at the edge of the park. Tess walked beside me as if she were wearing her harness – perhaps she didn't realise that she was not.

'Come, Tess – time to walk out into your new world.'

I stopped at the edge of the forestation and she continued to walk ahead. Just like that. Twice she looked back to see if Papi and I were coming, but when we did not, she vanished into the dense bush. I could not help my tears and Papi said nothing but gave me a long hug as we stood staring at the place where she had disappeared.

We got back into the Land Rover and left. What if she were to come back out after she had eaten? She might be afraid of being alone in the bush. We drove back to the farm, tears running down my face and Papi's hand reassuringly on my thigh when not changing gear, quite roughly I thought. It was late afternoon, her hunting time, and she was hungry, so I hoped she was doing just that and then settling under some low-hanging branches to eat and rest.

With no Tess by my bed, I didn't sleep well. Alone in my room, I confess I cried: my first night on the farm since she had come as a baby without having her sleeping on the floor by me. Pathetic, I know. I had always planned to leave Maforga the day after her release and I did – and would not return for about three months. I could not stay without her – she had been my life on the farm, always there.

When I came back at the beginning of February, it was still the rainy season, which I rather liked. Everything seemed to drip from the last shower and the world was lush and green. After tea and long conversations with Papi and Rosemarie about what I had been doing since my departure, I had an early night; naturally my first stop at dawn the next day would be Gorongosa.

In the morning I gathered Francisco, Rodrigo and half a duiker, one of Tess's favourites; I had sent a message ahead for the hunters to have one ready for me to take to her. They did not let me down. Papi was at the wheel, which was a blessing: none of us was as expert at driving on muddy bush tracks as my father. He drove with his usual verve with our two stalwarts standing up in the back of the Land Rover, ready to dig us out if we landed in a bog. I did not even look for game on the way – my thoughts were totally on Tess and what we would or would not find.

We arrived at the place where we had let her go, and the boys established a makeshift camp – we were planning to stay the night. I had made a recording of my special pattern of beeps from the Land Rover horn – a sound I knew Tess would recognise – and set up my tape recorder with new batteries and spares. Having placed the machine where we thought there would be the best acoustics, I played the beeps, followed by recordings of me blowing my whistle with the recorder turned up full volume. We waited. Ten, fifteen minutes, thirty minutes.

'She could be far away in this huge park,' Papi said reassuringly. 'She might hear and not want to come – or be hunting.'

Nothing. This time I called her: 'Te-ess; Te-ess', several times. Why would my voice reach her when the tape would not? Silly. We waited another ten, fifteen minutes. An hour. Nothing. Again and again I played the tape of me hooting the horn and calling her name. Then the whistle. Another hour.

Once four, almost five hours had elapsed, I was resigned to leaving the half-carcass in the straw lean-to and sat down, poking at the fire laid for the evening, chatting softly with Papi – when there she was. Not three metres away in long grass. Of course I recognised her: it could only be her, not another cheetah. She sat upright in her dog position. I wore khaki, the same scent as usual and as I called her softly, she trotted up as if I had never been gone, purring like a train, licking my fingers and head-butting my knees and thighs. I hugged her and noted how strong she felt. I always wore long sleeves – that mature tongue had sharp spikes and I was sure it could lick off my skin. She greeted Papi with a bump and a quick lashing out at his leg, a familiar play. Then she attacked the fresh carcass we had brought, obviously hungry but not starving. She did not look thin, which relieved me greatly, and while she ate, she allowed me to brush her and remove the ticks I found. She looked healthy and I was pleased there were only a few. I had to smile – Tess seemed to have settled in well to her new life – *better than I had into mine without her.* When she finished eating, we sat around an early campfire – any excuse to remain with her by my side for a little longer – but after another hour I could sense she wanted to be off again. After much demonstration of affection for us all, including Francisco and Rodrigo, she wandered towards the thicket. One last look around and she was gone.

We didn't stay. Instead we stamped out our fire and drove home in silence, without even the usual sound of the Africans chattering while standing outside in the back.

That evening we told everyone at the farm and those who came to the clinic how proud we were of our girl and talked until bedtime about her many funny little idiosyncrasies and adventures. I kept telling myself I had good reason to be happy. Tess's programmed future had come to pass. Papi and Rosemarie assured me that none of them, not Eduardo, not Benedita, had believed it would work. Either Tess would die before she reached adulthood or she would not survive in the bush. I did try to be happy for her freedom, but she had dug deep into my heart and I knew she would always stay there. It was just what Papi had warned me about on the day he put the tiny, sightless, hissing, spitting cub into my gloved hand. And it was one thing to have released her, but how long would she survive? She had never met another cheetah, let alone a leopard or a lion! The others thought of that, I did not. My sole concentration was on Tess and her reaction to her unknown surroundings. How I wanted to go back, call her, beg her forgiveness and then bring her back to the farm with me. Stupid, I know, but I couldn't help it.

Two days later I left the farm again. I had to get on and get busy with my own new life, comfortable and yet still anxious about having released Tess and desperate not to dwell on her, which I would surely do if I stayed. I kept meeting people who had reared or had experience of cheetahs – rather like having a new interest and then finding that every magazine or book one picks up seems to be about that one subject. The world I traversed seemed full of cheetah chat.

I could not return for another six months, but throughout that time I had regular news of the visits Papi, Rosemarie, Rodrigo, Assia and even Eduardo made to the place where we had released Tess. They brought her a part of a fresh carcass every time, including the offal to give her the vitamins she needed; played the tape recording I had made of my horn-hooting and whistle for her. Nothing. No sight of her. She did not appear. I worried.

This time when I came back to the farm and began to pack for our trip to base camp at dawn the next morning, Rosemarie decided she would accompany me; it was early August and the best possible weather, so driving in the rough countryside once we left the main road should be easier. It was only later that I realised Rosemarie's decision to come with me was because she felt better able to help with my heartbreak should Tess not appear. With no definite sighting of her during the six months I had been away, this was the most likely scenario: I learned later that Eduardo too worried secretly that we would find nothing this time. Thanks to our hunters, I had brought half a young reedbuck carcass with me, an animal too large for her to kill herself, but which she would love. Again I wore my old khaki with its familiar smells. Rosemarie was almost as good a driver in the bush as Papi, but happily we had no bogs to contend with.

The boys made camp and laid a fire ready to light in the evening. I settled down to the same routine – playing the tape, waiting, playing the tape, calling myself, waiting, more tape, waiting, calling. We had brought a picnic lunch and prepared it laboriously to kill time – we even found wild flowers and picked some to decorate the picnic table. We read the magazines I had brought with little interest, the tape playing non-stop.

The hours dragged by to supper time. It was more like a wake than a welcome home for me. After an early supper we sat around disconsolately, becoming resigned to the thought that she would not come – we had been calling and playing the tape all day and evening, ten hours or more. The day was ending and I thought we should stay the night to give Tess more time – perhaps she would come in the early morning, since that was her favourite time of day.

It was still light, but only just. In my heart, I made myself ready to go back to the farm and was about to suggest we clear up and put out the fire, when there she was – sitting silently, upright and solemn, watching us. Slowly I stood and called her softly: 'Te-ess, Te-ess, come on, my girl.' And she came, but hesitantly, as if not sure, looking over her shoulder – was she being followed, each step carefully placed? She appeared anxious, hunted almost. What was it? Was there a predator near? A lion?

The boys lit the lanterns while I stroked her, talking my usual silly baby-talk of reassurance, and she bumped and rubbed against me, but not in the same loving way – anxious, not purring. Then, to my surprise, she made her old familiar high-pitched chirrups, the same as she had when a cub. *Aiyhee! Aiyhee!* Short and sharp yelps, but soft. Was she reminding me of her time as a baby at home, sharing a memory? I brushed her, looked for ticks, found a few, murmuring to her she was safe, while she kept looking back the way she had come.

And then I saw them – two of them, fluffy, grey-beige, sitting, waiting, with just their little faces showing above the grass; eyes huge; black tear streaks clearly visible. I guessed they were about six or seven weeks old.

My breathing stopped, my heart pounded. I dared not move and nor did Rosemarie. I whispered, 'Clever girl,' as I had often done, and she bumped me, purring now, proud – and I imagined she knew how proud *we were of her.* She ate a little, and then turned back towards her cubs, calling a strange sort of *ihn-ihn*, and chirruping to them to give reassurance. Both bounced towards her and then she stopped and turned to look at me again. 'Oh what a clever Tess! What a clever girl!' Slowly I moved the carcass to the left of my seat, far enough away from the campfire and us so that she would eat – which she did, and then called them to join her. It is harder for a cheetah mother to make a kill with two small ones to care for, so I was delighted when after a while they came and tucked in, with all of us watching from a short distance. Tess was free, returned to the wild as Papi had ordered on that first day. To see 'my little family' looking strong and healthy, feeding and ignoring us, overwhelmed me with a sense of happiness that I will keep close to me forever.

Rosemarie and I sat there for about an hour until Tess called her cubs to follow her back into the bush, each with a little red from the carcass around their mouths and paws. Tess and I looked at one another – if only her eyes could speak. I made no move to touch her cubs: although I think she would have let me, it would not have been right. Her young were wild and should remain wild. Nor did I want to follow and find her lair – this was her life now, not mine.

We sat for another half-hour or so in silence and then broke camp to drive home, melancholy but happy too. Seeing her like this, I knew Tess had settled into her life in the wild. It filled me with both relief and joy, just as it broke my heart to see her again – and she had brought her cubs to show me! I knew that if she remained in Gorongosa, and kept away from the lions and leopards, she had the best chance of living and rearing her families, there where she was protected from hunters and poachers.

I decided then, and later told Papi and Rosemarie, that I would not go back to Gorongosa, never call her out again. We had chosen her life and it suited her. She did not belong to me nor to any of us who had reared her. Cats are domestic, cheetahs are not. Domestic cats are more attached to their home than to their owners and should be left there if the owners move, say some experts. Not wild cheetahs. They belong to the wild and, if moved, they can make a new home range. Tess had made hers.

Over the next few years, I often had news of her from the 'Tess Team': that they had been to leave food for her and had seen her with her cubs both grown. That she had come to the sound of the horn and been glad to take the carcass on offer. Once on safari, Papi was sure she had come alone to the tent, but that friendship had slipped into another phase and I had to accept that the experiment, although a success, was over... even if the memories will always be kept sacred in my heart.

EPILOGUE

Years passed, and although I buried her deep, I never forgot Tess. Raising her was not an experience I would recommend. I would dread anyone failing where, thanks to pure luck and good advisers, I had succeeded in returning a hand-reared cheetah to the wild. Already at that time I was aware of the trade in cheetah cubs, as well as other young wildlife: cheetahs are extraordinarily enchanting as cubs. Like everyone else who knew about this disgusting trade, I abhorred it and therefore did not talk about Tess in case it encouraged others to try to do the same. Most friends knew about some of my Africa experiences, but I tried to keep my cheetah to myself and my family circle.

In the 1970s I left Austria and moved to England, where I acquired two Siamese and two Burmese kittens (also two Labradors, which came to fear and respect the kittens, even more so when they became cats). I compared how they moved, stalked, attacked toys, how they would jump up high as Tess had done – sometimes she had even caught birds, but my cats wore bells. I bred a horse for myself to ride as a three-day-eventer and named her Vitesse – another Tess, with the same generous character and bursts of speed.

The story of my cheetah travelled quietly in Africa the way such stories do and, some twenty or so years ago, I was approached to help promote a centre for endangered species – predominantly cheetahs. How could I resist? Thus began my association with Lente Roode and the cheetahs she has bred so successfully at her Endangered Species Centre at Kapama in South Africa in order to release them into the wild. Like most of us who care about cheetahs, she knew how quickly their numbers were falling – during the twentieth century, the world population of cheetahs in the wild was reduced by a horrifying 90 per cent. This is due to habitat loss, attacks by lions and leopards, poaching, disease (often the result of their limited gene pool), scarcity of game for the cheetahs to hunt and angry farmers who shoot them as pests when they are found harassing livestock.

Cheetahs breed well in the wild but have always been famously difficult to breed in captivity, and although they are kept safe within very large areas at the Kapama centre, in essence, they are captive. Lente has devised a brilliant method of encouraging her females to breed. First of all, she told me, it is important to know the character of your cheetah. When she wants certain females to breed, she keeps them separate from the males – and one another – in large fenced-off areas facing a dirt road (privately called 'Lovers' Lane'). Next she encourages a group of male cheetahs to run up and down Lovers' Lane, which stimulates the females watching from their enclosures to come into oestrus. If a female has paid more attention to one of the male runners over another, he is put in with her and mating takes place. Should the female change her mind, her initial choice of partner is removed and another offered to her – until she decides on one of them! It seems that a female cheetah likes to *choose* her partner even if the actual mating ritual lasts only a very short time and takes place preferably in darkness or out of sight in dense foliage. The cheetah is discreet! Should a female dislike the partner presented to her and then be repeatedly offered another – as happens in some zoos – she will only become more stressed and mating will not occur. Lente's method has never failed!

The cheetahs released from Kapama wear a collar for satellite tracking, but that is often not enough, and at times a collar has been found without its cheetah. The area where she breeds her cats is too arid for farming, so that wild animals can have the range they need without coming face to face with livestock. But lions are breeding well and are numerous – and they kill adult cheetahs, as well as their young and their prey. Also poaching is increasing in the region where HESC is based and the search is on for more safe areas in which to release the cheetahs.

My dream was to bring some of the Kapama cheetahs to Gorongosa National Park. More than fifty years have passed since I released Tess there and Gorongosa needs cheetahs. They have lions and leopards, but not too many to prevent cheetahs staking out a territory. And Gorongosa is huge – there is room for all the cats. Could I send some from South Africa to realise my dream and have them thrive not far from the farm where I had brought up Tess? This idea danced about in my mind for some years and I made contact with various people who I believed could help with the transportation. Greg Carr, the American philanthropist, environmentalist and saviour of Gorongosa, was keen – and then the blow fell. I heard and had it confirmed that there is a resurgence of the old military conflict between the two original parties engaged in the Mozambique civil war – Renamo and Frelimo – and, worse, that Mount Gorongosa is the insurgents' base. Not a safe area, then, in which to release Kapama's precious cheetahs.

That must now be my quest – to find somewhere safe to release cheetahs in Africa where they can prosper and repopulate the countryside they once occupied. There *are* still places in the wild for cheetahs and we will find them.

Due to my involvement with Lente Roode and with another 'Cheetah Mother', Dr Laurie Marker, whose work I have had the chance to admire in Namibia, I began to see these elegant animals in a different way from the limited perspective I had had in my youth – that of caring for one vulnerable little cheetah which I raised inadvertently and which miraculously survived.

No cheetah is ever truly domestic: they are wild animals and can revert to their wild side. I have seen a hand-reared, apparently completely tame six-month-old cheetah attack a keeper from behind, leaping at her quite viciously and clinging to her back with what claws she still had. The keeper had broken a cardinal rule – never turn your back on a wild cat. But there are many similarities between a cheetah's behaviour and that of a domestic cat; teasing, for example – whether playing with a ribbon or with something alive which is food but which the cat may not necessarily even want to eat – is typical of both domestic cats and wild. Such behaviour is disturbing to many people, especially dog lovers, since torturing is something dogs do not do – and is a reason why many people dislike cats. I try never to forget that nature can appear cruel to our human way of thinking, although the only wild animal I have come across killing apparently for pleasure is the fox. And many people think Mr Fox is a most attractive creature! But talk to farmers in Namibia and they will curse the cheetah for taking young calves, goats or lambs, and then shoot it.

Statistics concerning the numbers of big cats left in the wild tell us of their dramatic decline in recent years. Every ten years or less we read of their populations decreasing at a rate that is hard to believe, and I know that the same can be said for many other wild species. Conservation groups do increase, which proves that there is concern, but still the big cats in the wild are disappearing fast and for a number of reasons. The main one is the demand for their territory – which is the fault of man.

Of all the larger cats, tigers are the most in danger of extinction, since there is no part of their bodies that is not alleged to promote healing or virility. I fear that this belief is so deeply ingrained in some people that it may be impossible to reverse and, within some twenty years, the only tigers in the world will be in zoos or similar establishments, no longer in the wild. My husband is involved with the tigers at Ranthambore National Park in India, as Patron of the David Shepherd Foundation, and also with the Amur tiger on the border of Russia and China, but the penalties for poaching are so low they do not discourage. As well as my work for cheetahs, I am the Patron of Mkomazi Rhino Reserve in Tanzania, a successful endeavour by Tony Fitzjohn which has recently become a national park. I pray the rhino has a future in the wild, but I am somewhat sceptical.

I know that many involved in conservation at times fear the worst, but we must try and continue to try. That is the message we have taught our children and they must teach theirs if they want to marvel at these magnificent creatures in the wild. The same can be said for many other wild species, I know, but I fear that in the next twenty to fifty years, the big cats will be seen only in conservation areas. Seeing tigers in the wild has been one of the greatest thrills of my life. I doubt my grandchildren will have that experience.

At Kapama there are several very rare 'king' cheetahs. They are a little bigger than 'normal' cheetahs and instead of spots, they have astonishing darker markings, whorls and blotchy patterns, often merging into one another like long black splotches, with three dark, wide, uneven stripes extending from their neck to their tail. This is the result of a recessive gene which must be present in both parents for another to be born, often only one in a litter. Although king cheetah skins had been seen earlier in the twentieth century, a live one was not photographed until 1974 in South Africa's Kruger National Park. Since then, more have been recorded and it has been decided that the king is a genetic variation of the common cheetah and not a separate species.

I saw my first king cheetah at Kapama about fifteen years ago (named Michael in honour of my husband). He was one of a litter of four hand-reared orphans, but only he had the markings designating him as a king. For a number of years I delighted in his attentions. I fondly imagined he remembered me whenever I visited – or else he had gracious manners. The lifespan of a wild cheetah is around ten to twelve years, although older ones have been recorded in captivity. The cheetah Michael has since died, but he lives on in the memory of all who remember his gentle, amenable ways.

At Kapama today there are eight kings, including two of which I am particularly fond; they are usually to be found in the large garden surrounding Lente Roode's house there. Male orphans called Nardus and Xander, they are the most loving young gentlemen, caressing and bumping my leg in greeting, or just licking the ends of my fingers while sitting upright. When I arrive at the gate I can hear them coming from some distance, their purr is so very loud!

I remember them when they were six months old, very affectionate and playful, climbing trees but having difficulty sliding down, as always at that age, playing ball and delighting in chewing my Argentinian capybara boots while these were still on my feet! They behave just like human twins in that they ape one another's positions so that they always appear to be shadowing one another, profile by profile, sitting side by side by the swimming pool, their paws hanging down. One day I found Nardus sitting on my bed in a sphinx position, gazing intently out of the window at the crowned cranes on the lawn. He had no business in my room, had not been invited in, but had managed to open the screen door with one of those clever paws that will bring down an antelope by snagging and tripping it with the dew claw. Cheeky is what young cheetahs are!

Although I do not see them from one year to the next, their reaction to me is always the same – as if I had never been away. Loud purring from a distance, front legs crossing each other as they swagger towards me, almost seductive! Then a bump with that wire-woolly head against my thighs, a finger-lick and a head placed in my hand. Nothing could be more flattering and I admit to being devoted. Just to admire a king cheetah's glorious markings is sufficient to enthral. For this reason Lente will never allow them to be released into the wild – they would not last long before someone coveted their stunning coats.

Something I have noticed with hand-reared cheetahs is that they empathise with human companions just as dogs and cats do. How is it that they know if one is sad or unwell? But they do, and they come and sympathise. Anyone who has cats and dogs to which they are close will swear the animals know when their master or mistress is coming home and will sit by the door or entrance, even after a long time apart. I was unable to visit Kapama for a year, during which time 'the king boys' had grown from six-month-old cubs to powerful subadults, but when I arrived nothing had changed. They snubbed me at first, but soon wanted to play.

When visiting Dr Laurie Marker at her Cheetah Conservation Fund (CCF) at Ojiwarongo in Namibia, my experiences have been somewhat different. According to the law in that country, they may not breed cheetahs. Their animals are brought in to them by farmers – perhaps cubs they have found after shooting a mother that was harassing their livestock. Even full-grown cheetahs have been brought in to Dr Laurie's centre for rehabilitation and eventual release. Others have arrived injured and these are carefully treated; then, if possible, released. Dr Laurie's aim is to have no captive cheetahs at the centre other than the few hand-reared orphans she calls her 'ambassadors' – animals used for training and education purposes.

Interestingly, these ambassador cheetahs are exercised by having them run chasing a tag attached to a wire driven electrically and at great speed – a more sophisticated version of what I did with Tess all those years ago. The older cheetahs know the game and usually two are set to run against one another. If they catch the tag, they receive a small piece of meat on a long ladle as a reward. But cheetahs are cunning, and if the tag is attached to a wire that runs in a circle, they will simply cut across the field to catch it on the diagonal. The operator also has to be clever and change the direction of the travelling tag, forcing the cheetah to double back until it pounces successfully. However, if unsuccessful, the cheetah may well just sit or even lie down, bored, exhausted and needing to wait for its blood pressure to lower. Another cheetah may not want to release its prize tag, and then I have witnessed a great deal of bribing with choice pieces of meat to make it let go. Rarely do two cheetahs follow the same lure: they seem to adopt the same idea of seniority as do dogs – or elephants for that matter. It is not even a question of size or age – just attitude.

Since I became the Royal Patron of the CCF in Namibia, I have renewed my trips to that beautiful country I first visited in 1962 when it was called Southwest Africa. Not long ago I was there with Dr Laurie and her team to watch her release three male cheetahs into a friend's substantial estate where there was room for them. It was fascinating to watch the big cats follow a vehicle towing a dead antelope out of the safety of their large enclosure and into the open countryside. Eventually, the carcass was released and the cheetahs dragged it under a bushy tree. Too excited to be hungry, perhaps, they nibbled at it a little, but seemed more interested in exploring their new 'home range', finding a 'playing tree' to read and learning from the scent an earlier passing cheetah had left there. From this a cheetah can determine the competition's age and strength. Also they were three, and he only one, so perhaps an older cheetah… all information for the new boys on the block to store away carefully while establishing a territory for themselves.

After a while, we left the three liberated boys to get on with their life – adventure seemed even more interesting than eating at this time. They each wore GPS collars and we knew we could find out if they had gone back to the carcass we had given them or abandoned it to other predators. Would they find more food? We worried a little – they were young and inexperienced and to leave a big, freshly killed antelope seemed foolish. With relief we heard that evening that all three had returned and eaten their donated kill, leaving – as always with cheetahs – a perfectly intact and clean skeleton.

One of the challenges with which Laurie Marker has had to struggle in Namibia is the age-old one of poaching, but in her case she also has to cope with the local farmers losing their cattle, sheep or goats to cheetahs. Naturally the cheetah finds a calf or a lamb easier prey than a fast, twisting antelope. Her solution is brilliant and seems to be working.

Dr Laurie met, approved and thereafter imported from Turkey, a number of large, gentle Anatolian Shepherd dogs. These animals – about 77–86 centimetres tall, the height of a Great Dane – are encouraged as young dogs to bond with the herds they are to protect. They have a very loud bark and would certainly stand up to a cheetah if challenged, but Dr Laurie hopes that will not happen: we know that the cheetah prefers smaller challenges and leaves the field in the case of a large one. Dr Laurie has now placed some six or seven hundred of these pups with farmers, with excellent results. The dogs are expensive, but if the farmers are unable to pay, means are found. In this clever way, farmers are learning to live alongside the cheetah, the only large predator their flocks encounter. Lions and leopards, I am told, have been 'removed' from Namibia – as have elephants – during the past hundred years.

During my many visits to Africa, I have observed the different relationships humans there have had with animals, mostly with the big cats and with elephants – so endearing with their prodigious memory and the sad expression in their eyes. I do believe elephants know they may be doomed to extinction in the wild, because of the lust in parts of the world for ivory. The same is true for rhinos, due to the strange conviction some peoples have of the therapeutic power of their crushed horns. I fear a similar fate for the big cats, also hunted for imagined 'medicinal' purposes or as trophies. How can anyone conceive themselves a hero for killing an animal with a high-powered rifle and a long-range sight? But they do, just as many people still believe in the curative powers of dried animal parts.

In Africa, I have witnessed and even experienced the healing powers of herbs used to make native medicines, but I cannot and will not condone the killing of animals to make any of them. Surely whatever part of an animal is supposed to possess remedial powers can be reproduced scientifically?

Nor will I condone the selling of cheetah cubs as pets, so often abandoned when their cuteness wears off and they become demanding carnivores. Or the sale of tame cheetahs, as I have witnessed in the Middle East, their claws and even sometimes their teeth removed. This disgusting trade in wild animals for human gratification must be stopped! The cheetah, that superb animal, built for speed and man's friend for centuries, has man as its greatest enemy. When I am protesting against the very practice of taming a wild animal for human pleasure, I often think about my own hand-reared orphan cheetah. But I did return her to the wild, and was content that she was back in her own element. And I did not take her from her mother, as unscrupulous people are doing with young cheetah cubs in Somalia, their mothers killed when they try to defend them so that the cubs become dependent on a bottle, then to be sold in Middle Eastern markets where they will not breed and the numbers will continue to decrease.

With so many native species declining in nature, I will pledge my continuing efforts to try to help at least one of them, the cheetah, to survive.

BIBLIOGRAPHY

Allsen, Thomas T. *The Royal Hunt in Eurasian History* (University of Pennsylvania Press, 2006)

Bottriell, Lena Godsall *King Cheetah: the Story of the Quest* (Brill, 1987)

Burke, S. M. *Akbar: the Greatest Mogul* (Coronet Books, 1981)

Divyabhanusinh *The End of a Trail: the Cheetah in India* (Oxford University Press India, 2002)

Hunter, Luke *Cheetah* (Struik Publishers, 2003)

Lloyd, Joan Barclay *African Animals in Renaissance Literature and Art* (Oxford University Press, 1972)

Robinson, Francis *The Mughal Emperors and the Islamic Dynasties of India, Iran And Central Asia 1206–1925* (Thames and Hudson, 2007)

Schimmel, Annemarie *The Empire of the Great Mughals: History, Art and Culture* (Reaktion Books, 2004)

Thackston, Wheeler M. (translator) *The Baburnama: Memoirs of Babur, Prince and Emperor* (Modern Library Classics, 2002)

Thapar, Valmik *Exotic Aliens: the Lion and the Cheetah in India* (Aleph Book Company, 2013)

Wrogemann, Nan *Cheetah Under the Sun* (McGraw-Hill, 1975)

ACKNOWLEDGEMENTS

First and foremost, I am most grateful to Jonathan and Angie Scott, 'the Big Cat people', who kindly allowed me to use their beautiful cheetah photographs and also wrote the Foreword. They are beacons of light and hope in the world of big cats and their conservation.

I would like to single out a number of conservationists to thank particularly for their advice and encouragement. The giant among them is Sir David Attenborough, whose documentaries are legendary and especially for his work about wild cats – I am indebted to him for his kind words. Another I want to thank for his personal advice and for taking the trouble to visit me is Gregory C Carr, who has made it his life's work to restore Gorongosa National Park in Mozambique, a place I knew well and which enters into this story. Gorongosa was utterly denuded of wildlife during that country's civil war in the 1970s and '80s and it is due to him that it has come a long way towards recovery. I would like also to express my thanks for the help I received from his assistant, Vasco Galante.

Saba Douglas-Hamilton, *Big Cat* TV presenter and renowned conservationist together with her family in Kenya, has been most generous with her encouragement, advice and endorsement. So, too, has Dr Sarah Durant, Head of the Range Wide Conservation Program for Cheetah and African Wild Dogs, ZSL and WCS – I'm grateful for her patience in answering my queries and for her illuminating replies. My thanks also to: Tony Fitzjohn of the George Adamson Wildlife Preservation Trust, another of my conservation heroes, who has been an inspiration and guide during his many years of active dedication to the wildlife in his care both in Tanzania and Kenya; Dr Luke Hunter for personally visiting me to brief me about the current situation in the cheetah's survival stakes – he and his books have been a great inspiration and help to me, as well as his organisation, PANTHERA, which he created to help all of the genus;

Lente Roode and her family for trusting me to be the Royal Patron of HESC, her Centre for Endangered Species, primarily cheetahs, at Kapama in northern South Africa and for allowing me to join in her work with her animals; Dr Laurie Marker of CCF, the Cheetah Conservation Fund in Namibia, for trusting me to be their Royal Patron and to see them in action releasing rescued, rehabilitated cheetahs into the wild.

I wish to declare my appreciation of Cheryl-Samantha Owen, Fellow – International League of Conservation Photographers (ILCP) and writer, for her energetic work and stimulus covering all aspects of photographic studies in aid of conservation. My admiration goes to Morad Tahbaz of the Persian Wildlife Foundation for helping to preserve Iran's tiny native wild cheetah population and gratitude for sharing his heroic experiences there. Richard Thomas at TRAFFIC deserves much approbation for his sterling work against the trade in wildlife, especially of still-suckling baby cheetahs captured in the wild, their mothers invariably killed by poachers. This trade must stop and I will do all I can to help end it.

Admiration and gratitude go to: Dr Rose Trevelyan of The Tropical Biology Association of Cambridge and Kenya, who has been a wonderful guide to me in the many aspects of conservation in her care; Ronald J Ulrich of the African Parks Foundation for his inspiration, friendship and for his great work; Jill, Duchess of Hamilton, dear friend and muse extraordinaire, who never fails me with either research advice or ideas; Ivor Ichikowitz of the Ichikowitz Family Foundation of South Africa for his immediate and generous response to my pleas for cheetah conservation support and for this book's promotion in his home country.

My grateful thanks to Simon Astaire, my far-sighted advisor in all aspects of public relations; to John Swannell for allowing me to use his beautiful photographs of me with cheetahs both on the cover and elsewhere in the book; to David Chancellor for joining me in South Africa to photograph cheetahs with me and doing so fearlessly!

Gratitude goes to Dr Amin Jaffer, brilliant expert in Asian art, who put me straight on a number of aspects of the Mughals and life with their cheetahs. For help with research into the Mughal heritage, I wish to thank especially Amanda Stebbings and her colleagues at the London Library; also Susan Strong and colleagues at the V&A library for images of Mughals hunting with cheetahs; and the kindness and efforts of Dee Vianna of the Royal Collection Trust.

My thanks go to Jean-Yves Ollivier and Paul Nicoli for having me to stay at their superb estate in Timbavati, South Africa, the better to observe cheetahs at Kapama and for the comfort and leisure to complete this book there.

I wish to voice much gratitude to dear friends Wilbur and Mokhiniso Rakhimova Smith for their encouragement, advice and for introducing me to Wilbur's literary agents, now mine, the excellent Kevin Conroy Scott of Tibor Jones & Associates and his assistants Laura Macdougall and Charlotte Maddox, who look after me there. They deserve my thanks for believing in me and in this book.

My sincere gratitude and appreciation also go to my publishers, Bradt Travel Guides Ltd, chosen for me by my agents; they have proved invaluable, especially Rachel Fielding, my editor Caroline Taggart and head of marketing and sales, Hugh Brune – all extremely clever and helpful.

I am deeply thankful for the work of my office in-house team – Camilla Rogers, Elsa Meagher and Joanna Hay.

Thank you too to cousin Johannes Auersperg for drawing the lovely cheetah logo.

Most of all, I wish to acknowledge the invaluable support of my husband – my first reader, guide and inspiration.

PHOTOGRAPHY CREDITS

The photographs of HRH Princess Michael of Kent and cubs, subadult and adult cheetahs taken at the Hoedspruit Endangered Species Centre in Kapama, South Africa and the Cheetah Conservation Fund in Otjiwarongo, Namibia are by kind permission of: John Swannell, David Chancellor, HRH Princess Michael of Kent, Lente Roode and the staff of the centres. Other photographic credits are:

Colour section 1:
p.1 B © Maggie Meyer / Shutterstock
pp.2–4 © Jonathan and Angela Scott

Colour section 2:
p.2 T © Christo Schreiber

Colour section 3:

p.1 T Ancient Egyptian fresco, 19th century. Artist: Ippolito Rosellini. Depiction of an Ancient Egyptian hunting party. From the collection of the Victoria and Albert Museum, London. Photo by Art Media / Print

p.1 BL Quadruped animals brought as tributes from the Tomb of Rekhmire – Vizier of Egypt, Plate XXII, from *The monuments of Egypt and Nubia: civil monuments, 1832–1844,* by Ippolito Rosellini (1800 1843). Photo by DeAgostini / G. Lovera / Getty Images

p.1 BR Two cheetahs wearing collars, formerly in a sketch-book *c.*1400. Brush drawing in watercolour and boycolour, on vellum. Anonymous. From Prints & Drawings collection © British Museum, London

p. 2 T Cheetah 'Acinonyx jubatus', from the 'Wellesley Albums', 1798–1805 (w/c on paper) / British Library, London, UK / © British Library Board. All Rights Reserved / Bridgeman Images

p. 2 B *Cheetah and Stag with Two Indians*, by George Stubbs, *c.* 1765, Peter Barritt/Alamy Stock Photo

p.3 Akbar hunts in the neighbourhood of Agra, by Dharmdas, by Basawan. Watercolour. Asia, 1590–1595. © Victoria and Albert Museum, London

p.4 *The Cavalcade of the Magi*, 1459, by Benozzo Gozzoli, fresco, Palazzo Medici-Riccardi, Florence. Photo by DeAgostini / G. Nimatallah / Getty Images

T = top of page TL = top left TR = top right B = bottom of page BL = Bottom left BR = Bottom right